p`ere Hyacinthe, Leonard Woolsey Bacon

Discourses on Various Occasions

p'ere Hyacinthe, Leonard Woolsey Bacon

Discourses on Various Occasions

ISBN/EAN: 9783744649094

Printed in Europe, USA, Canada, Australia, Japan

Cover: Foto ©Thomas Meinert / pixelio.de

More available books at **www.hansebooks.com**

DISCOURSES

ON VARIOUS OCCASIONS

BY THE REVEREND

FATHER HYACINTHE,

Late Superior of the Barefooted Carmelites of Paris, and Preacher of the Conferences of Notre Dame.

TRANSLATED BY

LEONARD WOOLSEY BACON,

PASTOR OF A CHURCH OF CHRIST IN BROOKLYN, N. Y.

WITH A BIOGRAPHICAL SKETCH.

NEW YORK:
G. P. PUTNAM & SON.
LONDON: S. LOW, SON & MARSTON.
1869.

Entered according to Act of Congress, in the year 1869,
By G. P. PUTNAM & SON,
In the Clerk's Office of the District Court of the United States for the Southern District of New York.

MESSIEURS :

Votre proposition de publier un volume de mes sermons et discours, traduits par le Rev. L. W. Bacon, ne saurait que m'être agréable.

J'autorise donc volontiers par cette lettre la publication de cette édition.

Veuillez agréer, messieurs, l'expression de mes sentiments distingués.

FR. HYACINTHE.

NEW YORK le 26 Octobre, 1869.

A Messieurs G. P. PUTNAM & SON, 661 Broadway.

GENTLEMEN :

Your proposition to publish a volume of my sermons and addresses, translated by the Rev. L. W. Bacon, is extremely gratifying to me.

It gives me pleasure hereby to authorize the publication of this edition.

Accept, gentlemen, the assurance of my highest esteem.

FR. HYACINTHE.

NEW YORK, October 26, 1869.

Messrs. G. P. PUTNAM & SON, 661 Broadway.

Stereotyped by LITTLE, RENNIE & CO.,
646 and 647 Broadway, N. Y.

PRESS OF
NEW YORK PRINTING COMPANY,
81, 83, and 85 Centre St., N. Y.

PREFACE.

THE following pages contain a translation, by the hand of a Protestant minister, of some of the most eloquent and powerful utterances of the Roman Catholic pulpit. They are translated with absolute honesty and fidelity—I will not say with elegance, for the work has been driven through at the utmost possible speed of the pen—and there has been no culling nor retrenchment to suit the volume to the American or the Protestant public. The only principle of selection and arrangement has been to take all the published works of Father Hyacinthe which I could find, in the order in which they came to hand, and bring them out in one volume, while waiting for an arrival from Paris for the materials for another.

I have no sort of apology to offer to any one for thus putting in wide circulation, among Protestants as well as Roman Catholics, these most charming discourses, which contain, with so much that will commend itself to the universal heart of Christendom, some things which I assuredly believe to be most serious errors. In the great impending controversy between the Roman-Catholic and Protestant systems, I, for one, would give every honest antagonist the opportunity of stating his own case in his own way. Whenever the result of this policy shall be to fix discussion upon the real issues between these great parties in the Church of Christ, instead of the factitious issues created by disputants on either side for the convenience of their argument, the cause of truth as well as of charity will be the gainer.

At the same time, it need hardly be said that these discourses,—though preached, some of them in the most prominent metropolitan pulpit in the Catholic world, under the auspices of church-dignitaries of eminent rank, by a monk of the austerest sect, and of standing then unquestioned,—are not to be taken as representatives of ordinary Roman Catholic preaching. To acknowledge this is simple justice, both to Father Hyacinthe, and to the Roman Catholic community, who themselves would decline to be judged by him as their representative. By their large-hearted sympathy with humanity in every rank and sect and nation; by a fervid Christian love, which attaches itself in the communion of saints to all who love the Lord Jesus Christ in sincerity; by a singular wealth and felicity of citation from the Holy Scriptures; by constant dwelling on themes of common interest to the Christian heart; by a silence which indicates little love for those things in modern Romanism from which the consciences of Protestant Christians shrink with most tenderness and pain; and by a most fiery courage in the denunciation of corruption, dishonesty, and Pharisaism;—these sermons are as exceptional in the pulpit-literature of the Roman Catholic Church, as they are exceptional in any literature by their splendid eloquence.

This volume has been hastened through the press to meet an immediate and urgent demand. But the value of it will not cease with the abatement of the local excitement connected with the visit of Father Hyacinthe to the United States. The subjects of the series of Notre Dame " Conferences" or Lectures, are peculiarly appropriate to our times and circumstances. The subjects of others of the discourses are interesting for all time and everywhere.

The failure of the health of an accomplished scholar, particularly versed in the intricate ecclesiastical history of France, who was to have contributed to this volume a Biographical and Critical Introduction, threw this part of the work, at the last moment, on my own overburdened hands. I have done the best with it that I could.

I present my acknowledgments, for the use of materials, to the Rev. Narcisse Cyr; to the Rev. E. A. Washburn, D. D.; and especially to my kind neighbor the Rev. Sylvester Malone, to whose library I am indebted for my first acquaintance with the writings of Father Hyacinthe.

For the patient kindness of Father Hyacinthe himself, who nevertheless is in no degree responsible for my work, it would be impossible for me adequately to express my gratitude.

LEONARD WOOLSEY BACON.

NEW ENGLAND CHURCH, *Brooklyn*,
November, 1869.

CONTENTS.

Letter of Father Hyacinthe to the Translator . . . xi
Biographical Sketch of Father Hyacinthe . . . xv
Letter to the General of the Order of Barefooted Carmelites xxxix
Speech before the Permanent International Peace League, Paris, July 10th, 1869 1
Reports of the Notre Dame Conferences of 1867, on Civil Society in its Relations with Christianity:
  I. Civil Society in its Relations with Domestic Society 17
  II. Sovereignty 40
  III. Religion in the Life of Nations 56
  IV. The Higher Intercourse between Nations . . 75
  V. War 90
  VI. Civilization 107
Sermon on the occasion of the Profession of Catholic Faith, and the First Communion, of a converted Protestant American Lady 123
Sermon on behalf of the Victims of the South American Earthquake 139
Letter prefixed to "The Select Works of Charles Loyson" 157
Appendix.—Men and Parties in the Catholic Church in France just before the Œcumenical Council, 1869 165

PREFATORY LETTER

FROM

FATHER HYACINTHE.

To the Rev. LEONARD W. BACON, Brooklyn:—

REVEREND SIR—I am as much gratified as surprised at the honor you are disposed to do to the few discourses I have published in Europe. Some of them are actually the production of my pen; but these are very few, and relate to circumstances of time and place which I fear will have no interest for American readers. The others, more important in their object, since they are part of the course of Conferences instituted at Notre Dame by the Archbishop of Paris, are extant only in detached parts, taken down hastily in short-hand, and the gaps filled by an imperfect summary.

I should have been glad, I acknowledge, if I could have brought to America something less unworthy of the sympathy with which I have been welcomed here, and which I shall always reckon among the greatest honors and the purest joys of my life.

Such as they are, however, I commit these rude productions to the indulgence of your readers. Frenchman and Catholic as I am, I present them, through your hands, to that great American republic of which you are a citizen, to those numerous and flourishing Protestant churches of which you are a minister.

I am proud of my France, but I deem it one of its most solid glories to have contributed to the independence of this noble country, which it has never ceased to love, and which it shall some day learn to imitate;—a people with which liberty is something else than a barren theory or a bloody practice; with which the cause of labor is never confounded with that of revolution, and never divorced from that of religion; and which, rearing under all forms and denominations its houses of prayer amid its houses of commerce and finance, crowns its noisy and productive week with the sweetness and majesty of its Lord's Day. "And on the seventh day it ends the work which it has made, and rests the seventh day from all its work which it has made."*

I remain faithful to my Church; and if I have lifted up my protest against the excesses which dishonor it and seem bent upon its ruin, you may measure the intensity of my love for it by the bitterness of my lamentation. When He who is in all things our Master and our Example armed himself with the scourge against the profaners of the Temple, his disciples remembered that it was written, "The zeal of thy house hath eaten

* Genesis, ii. 2.

me up." I remain faithful to my Church; but I am none the less sensible of the interest which will be taken in other churches in what I may say or do within the pale of Catholicism. And on the other hand, I have never deemed that the Christian communions separated from Rome were disinherited of the Holy Ghost, and without a part in the immense work of the preparation of the kingdom of God. In my intercourse with some of the most pious and learned of their members, I have experienced, in those depths of the soul where illusion is impossible, the unutterable blessing of the communion of saints. Whatever divides us externally in space and time, vanishes like a dream before that which unites us within,—the grace of the same God, the blood of the same Christ, the hopes of the same eternity. Whatever our prejudices, our alienations, or our irritations, under the eye of God, who seeth what we cannot see,—under his hand, which leadeth us whither we would not go,—we are all laboring in common for the upbuilding of that Church of the Future which shall be the Church of the Past in its original purity and beauty; but shall have gathered to itself, besides, the depth of its analyses, the breadth of its syntheses, the experience of its toils, its struggles, and its griefs through all these centuries.

In the sad days of schism and captivity, the word of the Lord came to the prophet Ezekiel, saying, "Thou son of man, take thee one stick, and write upon it, 'For Judah, and for the children of Israel his companions;' then take another stick, and write upon it, 'For Joseph, the stick of Ephraim, and all the house of Israel his companions;' and join them one to another into one stick, and they shall become one in thy hand."*

To me, likewise, who am the least of Christians, in those spiritual visions which are ever vouchsafed to longing souls, the Lord hath spoken. He hath placed in my hand these two sundered and withered branches—Rome and the children of Israel who follow her; the churches of the Reformation and the nations that are with them. I have pressed them together on my heart, and under the outpouring of my tears and prayers I have so joined them that henceforth they might make but one tree. But men have laughed to scorn my effort, seemingly so mad, and have asked of me, as of that ancient seer, "Wilt thou not show us what thou meanest by these things?"† And while I gaze upon that trunk so bare and mutilated, even now I seem to see the brilliant blossom and the savory fruit.

"One God, one faith, one baptism."

"And there shall be one flock and one shepherd."

BROTHER HYACINTHE.

HIGHLAND FALLS, ALL-SOULS DAY,
    Nov. 2, 1869.

Ezekiel, xxxvii. 16, 17.   † Ibid., 18.

BIOGRAPHICAL SKETCH.

WITHIN a very few years, we have been hearing, from time to time, of the fame of a great preacher of the Gospel that had risen up in France. Clad in the rough garb of a Carmelite friar, he has seemed (we were told) to be filled with "the spirit and power of Elijah." The sins of rulers and of people alike, the infidelity of philosophers, and the pharisaism of priests, he has denounced with equal and intrepid severity; and speaking in gentler tones to the families of his people, he has sought, like the predicted Elijah, to "turn the hearts of the fathers to the children, and the hearts of the children to the fathers, lest the Lord should come and smite the land with a curse."

The accounts of him have been as various, in some respects, as the strangely diverse channels through which they have come to us. In the innumerable crowds that have gathered within the sound of his voice about the pulpit of the venerable cathedral of Notre Dame, the most opposite classes have thronged each other, having no thought nor sentiment in common, save their eagerness to hear the great preacher. The bitter infidels of French liberalism, who listened to no other minister of any religion, gave respectful audience to him, as to a friend of the common people. The strangers and novelty-hunters of Paris sought at Notre Dame the revival of the palmiest days of French eloquence. Protestants of the austerest schools listened in that unwonted presence to discourses which, after every abatement of prejudice and of contrary conviction, they acknowledged to be the sincere and faithful preaching of Jesus Christ. And Roman Catholics of liberal sentiments justly gloried in the eloquence of their great preacher, and pointed him out as the living proof of the compatibility between Catholicism and the best spirit of the age. One party alone refused to join the general applause—it was the party of absolutism in State and Church; the Jesuitism that was resolved on crushing out the rising spirit of freedom among the earnest Catholics of France, under the heel of the Roman Court and Pontiff. But even those who hated the great preacher confessed his greatness. Those who hated, and those who admired, alike conceded the magnificence of his oratory, the earnestness of his convictions, and the heroic courage with which, in a land where it costs something to be thus courageous, he avowed them without fear or favor. Even those who had small appreciation of the distinctively Christian virtues could recognize in this poor monk more than the realization of the ideal of the heathen poet:

> "Justum et tenacem propositi virum,
> Non civium ardor prava jubentium,
> Nec vultus instantis tyranni,
> Mente quatit solida."

Suddenly, on the 20th of September, 1869, this foremost preacher of the whole Roman Catholic communion, declaring that he could no longer suffer with a good conscience the constraint which it was attempted to put upon him as a preacher of the gospel, retired from the cathedral pulpit, forsook the convent of his order, and in a letter which must ever be accounted among the memorable documents of ecclesiastical history, appealed from the authority of his monastic superior to the Œcumenical Council about to sit at Rome, and gave notice of his intention to carry the case, if need were, to a court of higher judicatory still—to the tribunal of Jesus Christ himself.

We are still too close to this great event, to estimate it in all its relations. Some of its consequences are so nigh at hand, and events are crowding so fast upon each other, that the boldest prophet might well hesitate to make predictions. The issue now on trial in the person of the Carmelite preacher is this—whether there is room and freedom in the Roman Catholic Church for a faithful preacher of Jesus Christ, who is also a docile student of the word of God, a denouncer of corruption, a hater of religious persecution, a friend of the universal education of the people, and a lover of human liberty. The common prejudices of Protestants, on this question, have been all ready to say No! The frank declaration of the extreme papal party is No! The great party of liberal Roman Catholics have hitherto said Yes! and have pointed in proof to the Carmelite preacher of righteousness and liberty and the word of God in the pulpit of Notre Dame. But now, what shall they say? This is one of the questions that is soon to be pending on appeal before the Œcumenical Council. The real friends of the Roman Catholic Church may well long for a decision in the interest of liberty.

Meanwhile, this illustrious preacher, following the most natural instinct of a confessor in the cause of freedom, has come to the United States. To the masses of our people, his lips are closed by reason of his foreign speech. This volume must be the pulpit from which he shall mainly address them. But before presenting his discourses to the reader, it is fit, in a few pages, to give such facts concerning his history as may serve, in some measure, as a personal introduction.

CHARLES LOYSON, since known to the whole world as *Father Hyacinthe*, was born at Orleans, on the tenth of March, 1827. His family was humble, his grandfather having been a harness-maker in the little city of Château Gontier, in the Department of Mayenne. But in the last generation, the family emerged from the obscurity of mechanical life into literary position. An uncle of Father Hyacinthe, bearing the same name, Charles Loyson, having graduated at the Normal School of Paris, became "*Maître des Conférences*" in that institution, and afterward, entering into public life at the new era which opened upon France in the year 1815, was chief of bureau in the Department of Justice. Among the companions of his education or of his too brief manhood, were such statesmen as de Serre, and Maine de Biran, such philosophers as Cousin, Jouffroy, and Royer-Collard, and such men of letters as the late Sainte Beuve, who all, with beautiful unanimity, have contributed to lay upon the early grave of their friend the homage of their admiration for his genius; while the illustrious Guizot, having outlived him to an extreme old age, remarked not long ago to his nephew and namesake, that there never passed two or three months without the memory of Charles Loyson coming before his mind.

The father of the great preacher, having achieved a liberal education, became Rector of an academy under the auspices of the University of France. When Charles was three years old, the family removed to the beautiful little provincial city of Pau, in the Department of the Lower Pyrenees. Here, in the midst of inspiring natural scenery, and of a population distinguished by many of the best virtues of country life, the character of the young orator was matured.

His education was in the seclusion of the family, his father's profession of teacher making it possible for him to enjoy at home more than the ordinary advantages of school. It was, he says, "a sort of family convent." The excellence of the instruction and discipline of this little cloister is attested, not only by the career of Father Hyacinthe, but by that of his younger brother, the Abbé J. Theodose Loyson, S. T. D., who now adorns the chair of "Evangelical Morality" in the Sorbonne with large and enlightened principles worthy of his kinship.*

Besides the scholastic and literary influences prevailing in the family of the Loysons, there were others of still greater importance. It was a Christian household, according to the best type of Catholic religion. The letter of Father Hyacinthe to the editor of his uncle's works, contained in this volume, indicates how the memory of that young statesman's Christian fidelity to right was cherished by his surviving kindred with greater affection than even the brief but brilliant record of his public career; and records, as a most precious heir-loom, the tradition of a saintly ancestor, who "through all the storm of the French Revolution had carried the lamp of God's word in her hand, or rather in her heart, without once letting it flicker or go out."

* An Inaugural Discourse by Professor Loyson, entitled "The Function of Reason in Theology" (*Du Rôle de la Raison dans la Théologie*), is published by Joseph Albanel, Paris.

Amid such influences of literature, of nature, and of religion, it is no wonder that the intellect, the emotions, and the faith were quickened and developed together in that symmetry of combination which constitutes the poet. In fact, the attention of the public was first attracted to him while he was yet in his boyhood, as one who gave promise, by more than one effusion of bright but immature genius, of fulfilling those hopes of a great poetic career which had been dashed by the early death of his lamented uncle. The general interest now concentrated upon him has led to the exhuming, from among old periodicals, of some of these early productions. The following, written by him when a lad of sixteen years old, and published in a newspaper at the time, has a proper place in this biography, as a picture of the beautiful surroundings of his child-life, and an illustration of the traits and tendencies already forming in his character.

SOUVENIRS D'ENFANCE.

"Dolce color d'oriental saffiro."—DANTE.

Lorsque j'étais encore un enfant frais et blond,
Que rien n'avait troublé le calme de mon front,
Mes jours, entre les jeux, la prière et l'étude,
S'écoulaient à l'écart et dans la solitude.

Notre maison était à côté d'un couvent,
Dans l'église duquel j'allais prier souvent.
Sainte-Ursule!—Ah! ce nom ranime en ma pensée
Le vivant souvenir d'une époque effacée,
Époque d'innocence, époque de bonheur,
Où mon âme portait tout son printemps en fleur!
Je t'aime! Et cependant tu n'as point, humble église,
De larges chapiteaux, ni d'élégante frise,
Ni d'ogive mystique aux vitreaux de couleur
Qui laissent pénétrer un demi-jour rêveur.
Je t'aime, et tu n'as point de dentelle de pierre,
De vieux murs tapissés par la mousse et le lierre,

Ni d'orgueilleuses tours dont les clochers joyeux
Plus haut que les oiseaux gazouillent dans les cieux.
Tu n'as point de tombeaux : les poussières glacées
Des morts n'attendent point sous les dalles usées.
Tes murs sont blancs, et tout en toi, riant séjour,
Nous apprend aussitôt que tu n'es que d'un jour.
Mais placé tout auprès de l'heureux monastère,
Où viennent expirer tous les bruits de la terre,
Quelque chose est en toi de chaste et de pensif
Qui calme doucement notre esprit convulsif.
Et puis de mon passé comme une ombre invisible
Te revêt à mes yeux d'un charme irrésistible !
Jadis, chaque matin, bien frais et bien lavé,
J'allais m'agenouiller sur ton large pavé,
Et le front tiède encor du baiser de ma mère,
J'adressais au Dieu bon ma naïve prière.
Que de fois, que de fois, aux offices du soir,
M'enivrant aux parfums qu'exhale l'encensoir,
J'ai senti lentement de ta voûte chérie
Descendre sur mon front la sainte rêverie,
Ange qui fait tourner nos regards vers le ciel,
Transformant par la foi l'idéal en réel,
Tandisqu'à la clarté des lampes et des cierges
Mourait et renaissait le chant voilé des vierges !
Comme un pain pur et blanc sur ma lèvre de feu,
Pour la première fois que je reçus mon Dieu,
C'était à tes autels, c'était dans ton enceinte,
Que pour nous avait lieu la solemnité sainte.
Voilà pourquoi je t'aime, et sous tes murs épais
Je viens chercher toujours le silence et la paix !

O temps évanoui ! temps aimé ! temps prospère !
Auprès du cabinet où travaillait mon père,
Dans une vaste salle où semblaient me garder
Des portraits ne cessant tous de me regarder,
Tandisque, frère et sœurs, je les entendais rire,
Sérieux, occupé de lire ou bien d'écrire,

J'errais de livre en livre, ainsi qu'en un jardin
Une abeille se pose et revole soudain.
Cette retraite avait pour moi le plus grand charme :
En y pensant, parfois, je verse quelques larmes.
Je la pourrais, je crois, dessiner traits pour traits,
Mais sans faire connaître hélas ! ces doux attraits.
Qui jusqu'au sein des jeux auxquels l'enfant se livre
Me faisaient soupirer après maint et maint livre.
Pourtant jamais l'ennui ne venait me saisir
Et me rendre pensif au milieu du plaisir,
Lorsque sur ces coteaux où Jurançon colore
Les raisins parfumés que son sol fait éclore,
Et dans une villa qui retrace à nos yeux
Les gothiques manoirs qu'aimaient tant nos aïeux,
Abri frais où jasaient de douces tourterelles
Et trois blanches enfants plus gracieuses qu'elles,
Pour partager ma joie et mes jeux innocents,
J'avais tout à la fois les oiseaux, les enfants.
L'ainée était pour moi la fille aux lèvres roses
Dont la bouche jetait les perles et les roses,
Ange, fée ou péri. Tout prenait promptement
Pour elle un air de joie et de contentement :
La brise lui faisait de charmantes caresses,
Et folle, se jouait avec ses blondes tresses ;
En glissant sur sa peau, le rayon de soleil
Y versait mollement un doux reflet vermeil ;
La brebis qui fuyait, si je voulais la prendre,
Accourait à sa voix et semblait la comprendre ;
Et le ramier craintif venait manger le grain
Qu'elle lui présentait dans le creux de sa main.
... Combien j'aurais voulu rendre plus lente l'heure
Qu'elle passait en ville et dans notre demeure !
Lorsqu'elle me quittait, je la suivais des yeux,
Triste et pensif alors, et naguère joyeux ;
Et bien longtemps après qu'elle était disparue,
Immobile toujours, je regardais la rue.

Puis tout me paraissait insipide, les ris,
Les jeux, l'étude même et mes livres chéris,
Tout m'ennuyait : en moi je sentais un grand vide,
Les objets avaient pris une teinte livide,
Et dans ces lieux déserts où j'errais jusqu'au soir
Sans cesse il me semblait et l'entendre et la voir.
Enfin, durant la nuit, amante du mensonge,
Son image venait me bercer dans un songe.

Un jour, un de ces jours où le ciel est si bleu
Qu'au fond de son azur on voit sourire Dieu,
Ou l'on entend monter sous sa coupole immense,
Un vague et saint concert d'amour et d'innocence,
Où la brise nous porte à travers les rameaux
L'haleine de la fleur et le chant des oiseaux,
Nous étions réunis par une douce fête
Qui faisait rayonner la gaieté sur ma tête.
Quand le soir suspendit notre jeu de cutin,
Nous allâmes goûter un champêtre festin ;
Et le long du coteau dont l'épaule se penche
Gracieuse et riante avec sa nappe blanche,
Nous trouvâmes la table à l'ombre, dans un bois
Dont l'écho répétait les éclats de nos voix.
On s'assit : mais hélas ! j'étais placé loin d'elle,
Et le temps nous parut d'une longueur mortelle !
Aussi, quand les enfants quittèrent le repas,
Nous retournâmes vite à nos joyeux ébats.
Comme un oiseau captif échappé de la cage,
Elle fuyait parmi les sentiers du bocage,
Et le taillis épais, à chaque vert détour,
La voilait à mes yeux, la montrait tour à tour.
Et je la poursuivais, comme dans la jeunesse
Le cœur, longtemps plongé dans une douce ivresse
Poursuit la vague et pure image du bonheur,
Qui fuit et reparaît à l'horizon trompeur !
J'avais douze ans, je crois : depuis cette soirée

Qui laissa dans mon âme une trace dorée,
Bien d'autres ont passé sans jamais affaiblir
L'éclat dont celle-là les fait toutes pâlir.
Oui, vous serez toujours mon bonheur et ma gloire ;
Rien ne vous ternira dans ma chaste mémoire,
O sacrés souvenirs que j'adore à genoux,
Et je resterai pur et vierge comme vous !

PAU, 22 février, 1843.

TRANSLATION.*

RECOLLECTIONS OF CHILDHOOD.

"Dolce color d'oriental saffiro."—DANTE

WHILE I was still a young child, fresh and fair,
With pure, calm brow beneath my sunny hair,
My days in study, prayer, and childish play,
In solitude untroubled passed away.

Our little house beside a convent stood,
Where oft I prayed before the Holy Rood.
Saint Ursula!—as the dear name I say,
Come thronging thoughts of years long passed away ;
When happy peace winged every fleeting hour,
And Spring within my soul burst into flower.
I love thee ! though within thy church's walls
The sunshine through no pictured window falls,
Making a twilight in the dreamy air ;
No stately nave or sculptured frieze is there.
I love thee ! though no dainty carvings line
Thy ancient walls, nor o'er them ivies twine ;
No proud bell-towers, whose chiming melodies
Outdo the birds that warble in the skies ;

---

* For the very felicitous translation of this poem, by Lucy Fountain, I am indebted to Putnam's Magazine for December.—L. W. B.

No pomp of tombs hast thou, wherein the dead
Low in the dust repose the weary head,
Within thy white walls all is bright and gay,
And tells us thou hast stood but for a day.
But placed beneath the happy convent's shade,
Where all earth's noises into silence fade,
Something within thee breathes a pensive calm
That falls upon the harassed mind like balm.
And like a shadow from my happy past,
A charm resistless round my soul has cast.
There, once each morning, on thy pavement wide,
I knelt me down, fresh from the limpid tide,
And with my mother's kiss warm on my brow,
My soul to God in childish prayer did bow.
How many times, while rose the vesper prayer,
And the swung censer perfumed all the air,
Descending slowly, like the holy dove,
A sacred reverie bathed my soul in love—
An angel sent to raise desponding eyes,
Where faith shows all they long for in the skies;
While the tall tapers gave a softened light,
And the veiled choir entranced the list'ning night.
Here, for the first time, were my footsteps led,
Where at thy altar, in the sacred bread,
My ardent lips upon my God were fed.
For this I love thee! Ever from thy walls
A holy peace upon my spirit falls.
—Oh happy days! O days long lost, still dear!
A lofty hall, my father working near,
I see among my early memories,
Where rows of portraits watched me with their eyes.
There my young sisters and my brother played,
While soberly from book to book I strayed;
Like the blithe bee that through the summer hours
Flits restless o'er the garden's wealth of flowers,
Lights on a bud and then away again,

I went from pen to book, and book to pen.
Ah, loved retreat, to memory ever dear!
The thought of thee brings the quick-coming tear;
E'en though I drew thine image line by line,
I cannot paint the spell that once was thine;
That through the mazes of our childish play
Still drew my soul to thy dear books away.
Then hand in hand with Joy my young soul strayed,
Nor ever met with Sorrow as we played
Where, on thy vine-clad hills, O Turançon,
The purple clusters ripen in the sun.
In the old villa, where our childish eyes
Saw Gothic towers in feudal pomp arise,
A cosy nest, where gentle turtle-doves
To three sweet children murmured low their loves—
I shared my sports, and spent my happy hours
With the bright group of children, birds, and flowers.
The eldest seemed that favored child of light
From whose red lips fell pearls and diamonds bright.
Angel or fairy seemed the vision splendid,
And peace and joy her every step attended.
The breezes followed her with sweet caresses,
And held their revels in her sunny tresses.
The sunshine there its lost gold seemed to seek,
And touched with richer rose her peachy cheek.
The lamb that fled before my outstretched hand
Ran to her call, and seemed to understand.
The timid sparrow lost its early dread,
And nibbled from her hand the crumbs of bread.
—. . . Ah, how I longed to stop the flying hours
When, in our home, we seemed to call her ours!
And when she left us, in my wistful eyes
The slow large tears of sorrow would arise,
As long I stood, with saddest discontent,
To watch, down the long street, the way she went
For in her absence all smiles fled away—

The charm had gone from study and from play.
A void was in my heart, forlorn and weary;
Without her presence all the day was dreary.
Through all my home, now but a desert drear,
Her form I saw, her voice I seemed to hear;
And through the watches of deceitful night,
Her image soothed me in a vision bright.
—One of those days when God's smile pierceth through
The summer sky, so perfect is the blue,
And to the vast dome of the arching skies
A hymn of love and worship seems to rise,
Mingling, beneath the shady forest bowers,
The song of birds and the sweet breath of flowers,
Out in the fields we held a little feast,
And her dear presence all my joy increased.
When evening came our wilder mirth to still,
Upon the shoulder of the little hill,
Within the dim edge of the echoing wood,
With smiling plenty heaped, our table stood.
Alas! between us yawned a distance wide,
And weary dragged the time, far from her side.

But when the feast was o'er, and we were free,
How blithely rang again our childish glee!
Like a wild bird let loose in native skies,
Through the green thickets swift her light foot flies,
And the chance turnings of the tangled maze
Now hide her form, now yield it to my gaze.
And I pursue, as wild with youthful bliss
We chase the flying steps of Happiness—
Vague form, that flies before our outstretched hands,
Then on the far horizon, guileful, stands.
My years were twelve; but still that happy eve
Within my heart a golden trace can leave;
And all the impressions later years have made,
Beside that bright spot into darkness fade.

Q Yes, ye are still my glory and my joy.
In my chaste thoughts naught baser shall alloy
The holy memories I still adore
With spirit pure and virgin evermore.

But while he was closeted in the seclusion of this "family convent," in the prosecution of solid classical studies, there was one door of his retreat that opened out upon a view of the great world of living questions and interests and men; and this was the library-door. The period of Father Hyacinthe's youth was a golden age in French literature. Jouffroy, on whom had fallen the mantle of Royer-Collard, was expounding and developing the philosophy of the Scotch school as against the debasing materialism of the previous generation; while Victor Cousin, with eloquence hardly paralleled in the chair of philosophy since the time of Plato, was delineating the philosophy of all schools and ages, and fascinating the students of other lands as well as France with his brilliant eclecticism. In the department of the higher politics, while the visionary schemes of the Socialists were giving daily and painful proof of the seriousness of the questions to be dealt with, Guizot, in the volumes of his Lectures on the History of Civilization, and de Tocqueville, in his unrivalled exposition of Democracy in America, were furnishing, from the past and from the present, the materials for their solution. In the firmament of religious literature, two greater lights shone so brightly on the vision of the young recluse at Pau, as to throw all others into obscurity. The first of these was Lacordaire, in whose person the broken succession of the illustrious preachers of France seemed to be renewed. Having the grace and earnestness to keep clear of "pulpit eloquence," he became, indeed, a great orator. Notwithstanding his monkish garb and discipline, he ever felt himself a man among men, and most of all when dealing with religious questions, for he dealt with them in their relations with men's current philosophies, feelings, doubts, aspirations, hopes. His wonder-working eloquence stirred the old vault of Notre Dame, and transformed the venerable cathedral from a lounging-place of tourists, and a haunt of straggling devotees, to a crowded forum of religious discussion, frequented by the most earnest men of Paris and the world. The other was the now venerable Count de Montalembert, the leader of those who, joining a religious enthusiasm for their native Church to an enthusiasm for liberty and native land, were laboring, in the face of ecclesiastical antecedents that might well have dismayed them, and of the Roman court that found it all too easy a task to crush them, to reconcile the highest obedience to the Roman See with true loyalty to the interests and rights of humanity.

It was mainly the influence of these two great writers over the growing mind of the young man at Pau, that seemed to determine his vocation to the priesthood. In 1846, at the age of nineteen, he entered the Seminary of St. Sulpice, at Paris, an institution for the training of secular priests. Among the faculty of instruction at the Seminary was one, the Abbé Baudry, to whose inspiring genius for metaphysical thought and instruction one pupil, at least, felt a debt of gratitude which he never failed to acknowledge, and which, in after years, he did what he could to requite by public eulogy upon his memory.*

After five years of preparation, Charles Loyson was ordained priest in the cathedral of Notre Dame. With that strong attraction toward an enthusiastic and successful pupil, with which faculties of instruction often seek to recruit their own strength and renew their youth, by devouring their offspring, the Company of the Priests of St. Sulpice attached to their own service the brilliant young graduate, and for six years he was employed, in almost entire seclusion from the world, in connection with their various institutions. Of this time, three years were spent in the capacity of professor of Theology at the Seminary at Avignon, two years in the professorship of Dogmatic Theology at Nantes, and one year as Vicar of St. Sulpice at Paris.

About the end of the year 1857, he withdrew from the Company

* The review of the "*Pensées Chrétiennes*" of Monseigneur Baudry, written by Father Hyacinthe for "*Le Correspondant*," will appear in the second volume of his Discourses.

of St. Sulpice, to enjoy one year—the last year, as it proved—of that domestic happiness from which his academic and monastic engagements have sequestered him almost all his life, but of the sweetness of which many of those discourses of his that were conceived in the loneliness of his convent-cell, show so tender and most human an appreciation. His thought was, in the repose of home, to ripen, by a few months of reflection, the fruits of so many years of unintermitted and laborious study.

At the beginning of 1839, his resolution was taken to enter the Order of the Barefooted Carmelite Friars; and in March of that year he was admitted into the Novitiate of Broussey, near Bordeaux.

That his decision to adopt the monastic life was dictated by no shallow or frivolous sentiment, and no worldly calculation, is clearly enough proved by the choice which he made of an Order. The original Order of Carmelites was one of the most austere in its discipline of all the mendicant orders of the Roman Church. But in the sixteenth century, that remarkable enthusiast and visionary, Saint Theresa, found that the ascetic practices which it required, under the "mitigated observance" allowed by sundry papal dispensations, were quite inadequate to satisfy the cravings of her soul for expiatory macerations and mystical meditations. In coöperation with a Carmelite friar, like-minded with herself, named John of the Cross, she instituted several religious houses, both monasteries and nunneries, in which the discipline was restored to the most rigid rule of the early days of hermitage. In her autobiography she speaks with special delight of the fidelity with which the monks of her first convent travelled about barefooted in the snow from village to village. At a later day, the rule of the order was so far mitigated as to allow a sandal, to protect the sole of the foot. But from this interdict of shoes and stockings, St. Theresa's reformed branch of the Carmelites took its name of The Discalceate, or Barefooted Friars. The monks are allowed no beds, but sleep on a board; and even such sleep as this is broken off every night at midnight by the summons to rise and say the midnight offices. No fire is allowed, save in the common hall. The fare in the refectory is of the plainest, no flesh being allowed throughout the year: besides this, throughout about eight months of the year, fasting is enjoined. The time of the monks is spent in a routine of solitary meditations and oral religious exercises; the ancient rule is: "*Maneant singuli in cellis suis, die ac nocte, in lege Domini meditantes:* "—" let every man remain in his cell, day and night, meditating in the law of the Lord." This, of course, is construed with some regard to the necessities of human nature; but in actual practice two hours each day of solitary meditation are exacted of the initiated.

The chief and primary object of the Order is contemplation. But a secondary and incidental object is preaching. And it may easily be believed that such a regimen as has been described, in the case of those robust constitutions which it does not break down, and those refined and energetic minds which it does not decoy into mere intellectual and spiritual indolence and sluggishness, may well result in producing great preachers. Certain it is, that when, two years after Charles Loyson had disappeared from the world behind the walls of the convent at Broussey, there emerged, in a pulpit at Lyons, the form of one Father Hyacinthe, the Catholic Church of France at once recognized its prophet.

If we pause now, for a moment, to look back on this career, it will hardly seem like the prophecy of world-famous achievements in the public preaching of the Gospel. Father Hyacinthe had lived for thirty-four years with the faculties and instincts of a great orator, of which it would seem impossible to be unconscious, growing and stirring within him, and yet up to this time his voice had never been lifted up in any more public discourse than that of a theological professor to his knot of students. We cannot but admire, either the self-restraint, or the power of ecclesiastical discipline, which could seal up, as with the seal of Solomon, in so small a vase, a genius which, once let the seal be broken, was to fill the world with its presence and influence.

If the question arises in any mind by what considerations such a man could have been induced to bind himself under the rigors of so austere and arbitrary and disabling a discipline, it will not be in the minds of those who have any acquaintance with the influences which, in a Roman Catholic community, surround persons of special devoutness of temper, to incline them to the monastic state. The traditionary interpretation and application of such texts as "Sell all that thou hast and give to the poor," "There be eunuchs which have made themselves eunuchs for the kingdom of heaven's sake," adds to these influences the semblance of a divine authority. And even the vow of absolute, unquestioning obedience to the will of a monastic superior, is made attractive, not only as an expiatory penance, but by the paradoxical conception that when all care and responsibility for the details of daily life is disposed of by one supreme act of self-renunciation, making it over to the control of another, the soul is thereby admitted to a true liberty. Such considerations as these, joined to that genuine love of secluded religious study and contemplation which his whole life had tended to develop, will explain, even in a country where such acts are unfamiliar, the "impulse of unworldly enthusiasm, mingled with illusions of youth," which divided the brilliant young professor of theology from family and friends, and bound him under the triple vow of poverty, chastity, and of an obedience to his superior in everything, limited only by the scruples of an honest conscience.

The first appearance of Father Hyacinthe as a preacher, in the city of Lyons, was attended by the same profound impression that has waited on all his public words from that day to this. After this commencement of his career at Lyons, he preached a series of Lent sermons at Bordeaux, in 1862; and the following year, being solicited by his former beloved instructor, the Abbé, at that time Bishop Baudry of Perigueux, to perform a like service in his cathedral, he went thither, but, instead of receiving the benediction of his venerated friend, he had but to utter words of grief and eulogy over his recent grave.

It was so lately as the summer of 1864 that Father Hyacinthe first preached to the world of Paris. This was in the church of La Madeleine. The deep impression resulting from his sermons led the Archbishop of Paris, Monseigneur Darboy, to send for the friar, and make a proposition to him from which almost any man might have been excused for shrinking with misgivings as to his capacity. It was that he should revive the Advent "Conferences of Notre Dame."

This word "Conferences," in this sense, is a new word in the vocabulary of the Roman Catholic Church. When the great Dominican, Lacordaire, in the last generation, felt called of God to vindicate for the Christian religion its right to a place in the France of the nineteenth century, he proposed to reach the ear of the French public, not by means of sermons, which they were habitually indisposed to attend upon, but by "Talks"—"Lectures," as we (using a word which in English has dropped its original meaning) would have called them. Associated with Lacordaire, the word *Conference* grew in the French language to be a synonym for manly, liberal, and Christian eloquence; and when, after the *coup d'état*, the congenial forces of political and ecclesiastical absolutism combined to shut his mouth and drive him to the fierce austerities of his monastic seclusion, there were still meetings and discourses at Notre Dame, but the Conferences were no more. The Lenten Conferences were maintained in form, but the Advent Conferences had been entirely suspended, waiting for another Lacordaire. The Archbishop proposed now to Father Hyacinthe that he should revive the Advent Conferences of Notre Dame, and the proposition was accepted. From that day to this, the preaching of these annual Lectures has been the chief function of the great preacher; and the naming of the subjects of them is the chief record of his life.

In the very first course, beginning December, 1864, the preacher opened his attack, fair and square, against the atheism of French society and of much of modern science and philosophy, with six Lectures on *A Personal God*.

In close sequence with this, the next winter, he undertook to exhibit the foundations of morality and of the authority of conscience, as resting upon God. This discussion was not only in consecutive relation with the preceding, but it was most opportune to the course of public thought when it was uttered. A movement which took on great airs of liberality and charity had begun to be popular in Paris, under the title of *La Morale Indépendante*, or "Independent Morality." The aim of it was to combine men in a sort of New Church, in which there should be neither Christ nor God, but only an absolute morality independent of all relations to truth and divine authority. Infidelity never puts on a fairer disguise than when, in rejecting Christ and God, it affects the virtues of Christianity. It was, therefore, a most timely service to Christianity when Father Hyacinthe stepped into the pulpit of Notre Dame, to be the champion of religion as the true foundation of morality.

Having proceeded from the doctrine of the personal God to the duty of man as an individual, the next step was to the relations of doctrine and duty,—in a word, of religion—to man in organized society. Following this course, the intrepid preacher boldly laid out before himself a course which must inevitably, if faithfully followed, bring him into collision with the sins of the public, of the government, and of the hierarchy; for he announced as the subjects of the next three years, the Relations of Christianity to Domestic Society, or the Family; to Civil Society, or the Nation; and to Religious Society, or the Church. These three courses of Conferences were commenced in December of the years 1866, 1867, and 1868; and at the close of the last course, in January, 1869, Father Hyacinthe descended the pulpit of the cathedral of Notre Dame, perhaps never to reënter it.

No abatement of the public interest, and no failure of the signs of a profound and salutary impression upon the vast audiences, suggested that the Conferences should cease, or be transferred to other hands. On the contrary, with each succeeding year, the impression of the preacher's words seemed deepening, and the renown of them widening. Neither was there dissatisfaction on the part of the eminent prelate who had opened to him the Cathedral pulpit. But another set of motives were at work, bringing to bear another set of influences, to embarrass and hinder the preacher in his duty. Year by year the language of the friar had been growing in boldness, and as in the order of his subjects he was drawn on to speak more and more pointedly of the sins of rulers and the sins of the hierarchy, it grew intolerable to those who felt the stroke of his invective, the pressure of his argument. There seemed little hope of redress from "the secular arm." Audacious as had been the rebukes which had been uttered from the pulpit of Notre Dame against the sins of the government, arbitrary as that government had been wont to be, in its dealings with free speech, it is simple justice to say that it never attempted to limit the liberty of this preacher. On the contrary, even the Emperor himself, "knowing that he was a just man and a holy, preserved him; and when he heard him, he did many things and heard him gladly."* For, to the great honor of the Emperor, the friar was invited to the Tuileries, to preach in the imperial presence. In fact, what could secular government do in the case? It is impossible to fine a man under a vow of poverty; and penal imprisonment could have few terrors for the inmate of a Carmelite convent. What then could be done? To complain to the Archbishop would have been vain, for that Gallican prelate of the old school was well known to bear little love to the complaining party, and not a little to the offending monk. But there was a third recourse, at once more easy, more certain, and more effective. And this was, to the discipline—absolute, autocratic, inexorable, claiming control both of soul and of body—the discipline of the Carmelite Order. The General of the Order resides at Rome, surrounded by the reactionary and despotic influences of which that unhappy city is the metropolis, and accessible to whisperings and accusations against his subordinates in every part of the world. The natural pride of such an Order in the fame of its most illustrious member might be an adequate defence against most charges, but not against so black and fatal a one as that of sympathy with popular liberty and education, hatred of Pharisaism, and a wide charity toward all true Christians, without as well as within the pale of his own Church. "Open attacks and secret misrepresentations" against the preacher of Notre Dame

---

* Story of the dealing of Herod with John the Baptist, Mark, vi. 20.

sought the ear of the General of the Order; but it was not until after the ears of the absolutists of Paris had tingled with the terrible concluding words of the last Conference of Notre Dame in January, 1869, that renewed against the Pharisaism of the nineteenth century the woes uttered by our Lord against that of the first century, that "the intrigues of a party omnipotent at Rome" at last succeeded.*

The convenient occasion for the rebuke and punishment of Father Hyacinthe was not long to seek. On the tenth of July, 1869, was held a meeting, in Paris, of the "Permanent International Peace League," a society of liberals in politics, assembled to devise means for the preservation of that which long and bloody history has satisfied all liberal minds in Europe is the best hope of liberty for the people—civil and international peace. Doubtless it was a strange place and platform for a Carmelite friar. French liberals are not, as a class, very orthodox, nor very religious, and especially not very Catholic. On the other hand, Catholic priests, as a class, are not very liberal. It is both pitiful and true, that love of freedom and progress and humanity, in Europe, and especially in France, is largely identified with infidelity; and that, while Christianity is identified with Catholicism in the popular mind of France, Catholicism (as a whole) is inextricably implicated with "Cesarism" and enmity to popular liberty and rights. It was a step in advance of Lacordaire, when Father Hyacinthe took his place on the rostrum of the Peace League. Lacordaire had brought the infidels to the church to hear the vindication of religion. Hyacinthe carried the gospel to the very

---

* The concluding paragraphs of this invective are contained in the article, by De Pressensé, appended to this volume. The words, with all the discourses which they conclude, were preached in Rome, in the Lent of 1868, in the church of "St. Louis of the French," to throngs of Frenchmen, and other foreigners, and seemed to be heard with universal respect; and at the close of the series, the preacher was received by the Pope with every testimony of honor and good-will. But when, at the next Advent, the same words were repeated before the Ultramontanes of Paris, "they perceived that he spake of them," and took counsel from that hour more effectually to silence him.

council chamber of "liberalism," and there vindicated his Saviour and ours as being the Peacemaker of the world.

Those who read this marvellous speech in the subsequent pages of this volume, will find reason enough why infidelity might have been enraged to listen to it; and reason enough why the "personal government" of the Cesar of France might have burned to avenge itself upon the preacher; but they will look, and wonder, and look again, to see what scruple the friends of the gospel and the church, even taking this latter word in its narrowest sense of an external corporation, could have had at this vindication of Christ among unbelievers. And yet the government listened to this fatal invective* with patient, though profound dissatisfaction. Infidelity had nothing but admiration for the brave priest who had attacked it to its face. Those who denounced him were the representatives of the religion which he had defended, and of the Christ whom he had vindicated. Strangely enough, the passage of the speech on which they fastened their accusations was that eulogy on the word of God as the true source of genuine light and civilization, in which the preacher declares that those three communions only which derive their principles from that word— Judaism, Protestantism, Catholicism—are able to bear the daylight of modern civilization. For this the party of absolutism gnashed upon him with their teeth, declaring that he had "crucified the Catholic Church between two thieves." Under the pressure of a chorus of indignant complaints, open and secret, the support of the Carmelite General, which hitherto had never failed Father Hyacinthe, at last gave way. A sharp rebuke was administered to him, condemning his course as a preacher, and requiring him thenceforth to refrain from addressing secular assemblies, and, in the pulpit, to restrict himself to the points on which all Catholics were agreed.

After all, the fault was not so much in anything he had said at this time, as in what he was, and that his time had come. Those

* The speech before the Peace League was pronounced considerably before that meeting of the French Legislature in which the attack upon "personal government" was renewed in the bitter interpellations of the liberals.

who had narrowly observed his preaching, whether as friends or as foes, perceived distinctly how it all tended to three principal ends:

1. To take up and carry on the great work of Lacordaire, of reconciling the Roman Catholic Church with Modern Society.

2. Not by compromise of convictions, but by the points of common belief and practice, and by the spirit of peace and charity, to draw toward each other the various communions of Christian believers; and to develop and set forth before the people the doctrine of "the soul of the Church," which is really common alike to the Roman and to the Protestant theology:—that they are not all of the church who are in the church; and that, on the other hand, they are not all outside of "the soul of the church" who are outside its visible pale; but that the one universal sign of true discipleship is "this sign, that the Lord knoweth them that are his."

3. To endeavor to bring back the Roman Catholic Church toward the spirit of its early days.

The real question was whether a preacher having these aims could have liberty of speech within the Roman priesthood. This question, decided in the negative in the court of first resort, is now pending before the highest tribunal of the Roman Church. But while that question waits for its final answer, it is not the monk that is on trial, but the Church.

It remains to add here the document on which the case is carried up. It might have been thought fit to include it among the *writings* of its author which follow it. But it is better here, as a great act of his life; a memorable fact in the history of the Church of Jesus Christ; "a word"—as one has said before, of utterances as brave as this—"a word which is a half-battle."

LETTER OF FATHER HYACINTHE TO THE GENERAL OF HIS ORDER.

To the Reverend, the General of the Order of Barefooted Carmelites, Rome:

Very Reverend Father:—

During the five years of my ministry at Notre Dame, Paris, notwithstanding the open attacks and secret misrepresentations of which I have been the object, your confidence and esteem have never for a moment failed me. I retain numerous testimonials of this, written by your own hand, and which relate as well to my preaching as to myself. Whatever may occur, I shall keep this in grateful remembrance.

To-day, however, by a sudden shift, the cause of which I do not look for in your heart, but in the intrigues of a party omnipotent at Rome, you find fault with what you have encouraged, blame what you have approved, and demand that I shall make use of such language, or preserve such a silence, as would no longer be the entire and loyal expression of my conscience.

I do not hesitate a moment. With speech falsified by an order from my superior, or mutilated by enforced reticences, I could not again enter the pulpit of Notre

Dame. I express my regrets for this to the intelligent and courageous bishop, who placed me and has maintained me in it against the ill-will of the men of whom I have just been speaking. I express my regrets for it to the imposing audience which there surrounded me with its attention, its sympathies—I had almost said, with its friendship. I should be worthy neither of the audience, nor of the bishop, nor of my conscience, nor of God, if I could consent to play such a part in their presence.

I withdraw at the same time from the convent in which I dwell, and which, in the new circumstances which have befallen me, has become to me a prison of the soul. In acting thus I am not unfaithful to my vows. I have promised monastic obedience—but within the limits of an honest conscience, and of the dignity of my person and ministry. I have promised it under favor of that higher law of justice, the "royal law of liberty," which is, according to the apostle James, the proper law of the Christian.

It was the most untrammelled enjoyment of this holy liberty that I came to seek in the cloister, now more than ten years ago, under the impulse of an enthusiasm pure from all worldly calculation—I dare not add, free from all youthful illusion. If, in return for my sacrifices, I to-day am offered chains, it is not merely my right, it is my duty to reject them.

This is a solemn hour. The Church is passing through one of the most violent crises—one of the darkest and most decisive—of its earthly existence. For the first time in three hundred years, an Œcumenical Council is not only summoned, but declared necessary. These are the expressions of the Holy Father. It is not at such a moment that a preacher of the Gospel, were he the least of all, can consent to hold his peace, like the "dumb dogs" of Israel—treacherous guardians, whom the prophet reproaches because they could not bark. *Canes muti, non valentes latrare.*

The saints are never dumb. I am not one of them, but I nevertheless know that I am come of that stock—*filii sanctorum sumus*—and it has ever been my ambition to place my steps, my tears, and, if need were, my blood, in the footprints where they have left theirs.

I lift up, then, before the Holy Father and before the Council, my protest as a Christian and a priest against those doctrines and practices, which call themselves Roman, but are not Christian, and which, making encroachments ever bolder and more deadly, tend to change the constitution of the Church, the substance, as well as the form of its teaching, and even the spirit of its piety. I protest against the divorce, not less impious than mad, which men are struggling to accomplish between the Church, which is our mother for eternity and the society of the nineteenth century, whose sons we are for time, and toward which we have also both duties and affections.

I protest against that opposition, more radical and frightful yet, which sets itself against human nature, attacked and revolted by these false teachers in its most indestructible and holiest aspirations. I protest above all against the sacrilegious perversion of the Gospel of the Son of God himself, the spirit and the letter of which, alike, are trodden under foot by the Pharisaism of the new law.

It is my most profound conviction, that if France in particular, and the Latin races in general, are delivered over to anarchy, social, moral and religious, the principal cause of it is to be found—not, certainly, in Catholicism itself—but in the way in which Catholicism has for a long time past been understood and practised.

I appeal to the Council now about to assemble, to seek remedies for our excessive evils, and to apply them alike with energy and gentleness. But if fears which I am loth to share, should come to be realized—if that august assembly should have no more of liberty in its deliberations than it has already in its preparation—if, in one word, it should be robbed of the characteristics essential to an Œcumenical Council, I would cry to God and men to demand another, really assembled in the Holy Spirit, not in the spirit of party—really representing the church universal, not the silence of some and the constraint of others. "For the hurt of the daughter of my people am I hurt. I am black. Astonishment hath taken hold on me. Is there no balm in Gilead—is there no physician there? Why then is not the health of the daughter of my people recovered?"—*Jeremiah*, viii. 21, 22.

And, finally, I appeal to Thy tribunal, O Lord Jesus! *Ad tuum, Domine Jesu, tribunal appello.* It is in Thy presence that I write these lines; it is at Thy feet, after having prayed much, pondered much, suffered much, and waited long—it is at Thy feet that I subscribe them. I have this confidence concerning them, that, however men may condemn them upon earth, Thou wilt approve them in heaven. Living or dying, this is enough for me.

BROTHER HYACINTHE,

Superior of the Barefooted Carmelites of Paris, Second Definitor of the Order in the province of Avignon.

PARIS—PASSY, September 20, 1869.

The answer to this letter was everything that the enemies of the preacher of righteousness desired. It was a peremptory summons from the General of the Order, to betake himself to one of the convents of the Order in the south of France, within ten days, under pain of excommunication from the Catholic Church, accompanied with "the mark of infamy." When the ten days had expired, Father Hyacinthe was on his way to the United States of America.

He has come hither an excommunicated member of the Roman Church, but still a member. The doctrines which he has learned in her schools and preached in her pulpits, he has not repudiated. The conception of the future union of all Christian souls in the organic and visible fellowship of her communion, he still cherishes with most filial affection. But from that communion he himself is cast out. Before the law and the hierarchy of the Church, he is an excommunicate.

But before God and his own conscience? Not at all. The doctrine of Roman theology, that absolution looses the soul only when contrition is sincere (which the priest does not undertake certainly to know), is complemented by the doctrine equally settled, that excommunication binds the soul only when the offence charged is actual, of which the hierarch is no infallible judge.* Bearing, within, a conscience void of offence before God, he may walk amid the falling thunderbolts of Rome unhurt, and "fear no evil, for the Lord is with him."

* The famous theologian, Passaglia, I am told, has discussed the subject of excommunication in this sense, in terms which were deemed offensive by the Roman party in the Roman Church; but I have not had time to find his pamphlet.

DISCOURSES

OF THE REVEREND

FATHER HYACINTHE.

SPEECH BEFORE THE PEACE LEAGUE AT PARIS, JULY 10, 1869.

LADIES AND GENTLEMEN: I have only a few words to add to the learned and eloquent speeches to which you have been listening. After such voices, mine can have but little weight in these matters. Its sole importance is, that it more directly represents among you the gospel.

The Permanent International Peace League proposes to act on public opinion by every means; and resorts accordingly to whatever light may illuminate it, and whatever force is competent to guide it. Among these lights and forces it must place in the front rank the gospel, a light so pure, a force so potent, that not even the feebleness of our words nor the humbleness of our persons can weaken or obscure it.

For my part, then, I bring to the peace movement *the gospel;* not that gospel dreamed of by sectaries of every age—as narrow as their own hearts and minds— but my own gospel, received by me from the Church and from Jesus Christ, a gospel which claims authority over everything and excludes nothing—[*sensation*]—

which reiterates and fulfils the word of the Master, "he that is not against us is for us," and which, instead of rejecting the hand stretched out to it, marches forward to the van of all just ideas and all honest souls. [*Applause.*]

Permit me, then, before exhibiting religion and virtue as the best safeguards of peace, to recognize the services which may be rendered to it by institutions and interests of a more earthly sort. Institutions, Interests, Virtues—these are the instruments of peace on which I would fix your attention.

I. I have named Institutions first. Perhaps it is a mistake; for when we ask ourselves thoughtfully what sort of institutions would be adapted to secure the peace of the world, we come upon ideas so little practical that we seem to have reached the region of chimeras. I scarcely see any effectual institution other than that of a sovereign international court of justice, commissioned to adjudicate the disagreements arising among nations, and by authoritative judgments to prevent bloody collision. The future, perhaps, will enjoy such an institution. I am one of those who believe all the more in progress because of the entire faith we have in the gospel, in redemption, in all those supernatural influences brought into the world, directly—principally, doubtless, to save souls, but also, as an inevitable and glorious incident, to save nations and the whole body of mankind. [*Cries of Bravo.*] Possibly, in a future more or less remote, our posterity may salute that grand Areopagus which would realize in this part of the continent something like what has been spoken of as "the United States of Europe;" but that is not to be to-day nor to-morrow; and consequently such an institution could not be reckoned among the barriers which we would oppose to war.

I recur rather to two powers now existing; diplomacy, representing the governments—and opinion, representing the people. It devolves on diplomacy and on public opinion, rising to the grandeur of that mission which the will of God and the conscience of mankind have appointed to them, to oppose insurmountable obstacles to the invasion of this scourge. Let diplomacy renounce the spirit as well as the letter of Machiavelli, let it reject the false science of expedients, the mean arts of deceit, and illuminated by the grand light of principles, glowing with the flame of generous sentiments, it will speedily have established in all the great centres of Europe an international league, a permanent and sovereign council of peace. But why speak of Europe only, when from the depths of Asia, over the crumbling battlements of the great wall, I hear that old China is sending us the son of youthful America, and claiming, through her representative, the honor of a place among civilized nations. This is the sort of diplomacy which has indeed the secret of the future!

But, after all, it is less to diplomacy than to public opinion that we must have recourse for our projects of peace. Pascal says, "Opinion is the queen of the world; force is but its tyrant." It was but the morning twilight of public opinion that was shining in the days of Pascal and Louis XIV. The morning has advanced since then; it approaches its meridian, and everywhere, to-day, it tends to put an end to the caprices of personal government. [*Bravo! Bravo! Enthusiastic shouts.*]

Personal governments have had their reason and their uses in other ages. [*Smiles. Good! good!*] A child stands in need of masters and tutors of a very personal sort; but, as St. Paul says, speaking of regenerate humanity, we are no longer children nor slaves; we are entitled to come into possession of the inheritance. It is no time now for personal governments. [*Applause.*] It is time for the government of public opinion, for the government of the country by itself; and now that all countries are calling and stretching out the hand to one another, the hour is at hand for the government of mankind by itself.

I put the question, What is it that the nations demand to-day? Is it war, or peace? From the shores of America to those of Europe, and from all lands of the earth, there comes up a great cry that answers, Peace! Mankind (as was said in the speech to which we have just listened), mankind to-day more than ever feels that it is one; faithful to its several members, to particular countries, it sees above these countries the universal country, that commonwealth of God and man of which Cicero spoke: "*Universus hic mundus, una civitas communis Deorum atque hominum.*" Mankind is conscious that every war within itself is a civil war; it has no wish to be henceforth a camp, but a forum and a market, and over these a temple, whither it may ascend to worship God. [*Applause.*]

Ladies and Gentlemen, I had almost forgotten an institution for which (as our honorable Secretary seems disposed to remind you), I have been accused, in other circumstances, of having had some partiality—I mean the army. I believe that, properly restricted and properly organized, the army is one of the most potent instruments of peace. The pure type of the soldier seems to me, in the epoch in which we live, almost as necessary to civilization as that of the priest; and I should be extremely sorry not to do justice to it. I do not speak of those monstrous armies born in days of fever, under the influence of vertigo, and which, making of peace a scourge almost as terrible as war itself, dig under the tramp of their ponderous battalions bottomless pits in the finances of the State, in the prosperity of families, in the blood of such multitudes of young men made sterile or corrupt. [*Lively approbation.*] Surely I have no admiration for that; and when Europe wakes, at last, from this bad dream which she has been dreaming for some years, not content with effacing such scandals from her laws and usages, she will blush that she cannot also expunge them from her history. What we want is the army reduced to its legitimate proportions; withdrawn in time of peace from the corrupting life of the garrison, and organized in such wise as to find its greatest satisfaction in peace. We have been told of the six thousand men who constitute the effective force of the United States. [*Smiles.*] I do not think that we are far enough advanced toward the future to be satisfied with that. [*Marks of assent.*] But we have on the old continent other examples more in correspondence with our social condition, which we shall do well, I will not say to copy, but to imitate with originality and independence. In the better part of Europe, the soldier is less isolated than with us from family and country life. It is in cultivating the soil, in dwelling by the fireside, that he learns to love them and defend them. *Pro aris et focis.* But why look beyond ourselves? Have we forgotten the first wars of our own republic, and those levies in mass to save the country, and those armies of undrilled peasants, oftentimes without shoes and without bread, who went forth to cover the frontier with a belt of heroic hearts, that they might hide from the eye of the stranger the shame within—

the scaffold and the saturnalia—and that they might hurl back the veteran armies of all Europe in league against us?

II. I have a word to say concerning Interests. Earthly interests are a great matter—full of ideas and virtues; and after all, when God puts us on the earth, it is not to dream about heaven, but to prepare for it. [*Good! good!*] It is by the conquest of earth that man should advance to the conquest of heaven. The holy Book tells that God in his wisdom has made man to establish this world in justice and truth.* These are words which we cannot too often ponder; most of all, we cannot too closely apply them.

Ladies and Gentlemen, the justice which man owes the earth is agriculture, industry, commerce. Agriculture holds the foremost place. The earth lies in a lethargic slumber till it is roused by the stout arm of the laborer. It imbibes the sweat of man's brow, and becomes intoxicated with those bitter and sacred drops; it becomes disgusted at its native barbarism, and yields itself, actively and gladly, to the transforming and fertilizing culture. So the earth, established in justice and truth, becomes the fostermother of multitudes, opening her generous breasts to men of every nation, and pouring out to them those great streams of physical life without which moral life itself would speedily die away. The farmer with worthy pride turns over to the artisan the product of his labor, and says, Brother, complete my work and begin your own! pursue the great toil prescribed by God to man. And the artisan takes the fruits of agriculture, summons from every quarter the hidden or refractory powers of nature, subdues the refractory, brings to light the hidden, and in his turn creates those wonders which are the last utterance of man and of

* Wisdom, ix. 2, 3.

matter in the sphere of the useful, as the fine arts are their last utterance in the sphere of the beautiful. And when farmer and artisan have done their work, then commerce lifts her broad wings, her sails fill, her engines hiss and throb, her ships plough the sea, her fiery chariots traverse the land, the arteries of nations open in every direction, that the blood of a common civilization, the vivifying sap of the same moral ideas and the same material products, may permeate all mankind. And the word of Saint Paul is fulfilled, which was not made known before the coming of Christianity, that supreme inspirer of great things, *Gentes esse cohæredes*, "that the nations should be fellow-heirs."

Now, Ladies and Gentlemen, what is it but peace, that stands, with Christianity, at the beginning and at the end of all these things? Peace as origin and result; peace always and everywhere! Woe, woe, if the war-trumpet sounds, if the arms of laborers in field and workshop are turned violently from their proper object, if the sails of the merchant-ships are suddenly furled, and if, alike by land and sea, instead of the glad din of labor, we hear only the fearful shock of destruction! [*General signs of approval.*] Away with these hateful images! Let us pause a moment before two great spectacles of the passing hour.

You are Christians. I also am a Christian, and a priest, and a monk. But neither in the Christian religion, nor in these glorious rags of the monastic habit, nor in the seclusion of cloister and temple, has it been in my wish, nor in my power, to sever myself from interest in the things of earth! [*Good! good!*] Accordingly, Ladies and Gentlemen, it is with genuine emotion, that in behalf of you all, I hail these new triumphs of human toil and genius!

I turn toward the East, whence morning by morning comes the sun, whence comes the light of the gospel, and at the point which once divided Europe and Asia, I see no longer division, but the sign of glorious union. It is the admiration and advantage of the world; but it is the work of France. My France has wrought it! [*Cries of Bravo.*] France conceived the project; she maintained it against the sneers which are the portion of genius as well as of virtue; she invented those prodigious machines, and made the rocks, as the Psalmist says, "to leap like rams," and sends gliding and sparkling through the sunshine of the desert the waters of the canal that is to join two worlds!

I turn now to the West. This time it is the water which divides—the vast Atlantic, rolling between America and us. But see, from the lofty decks of the glorious Leviathan, in our harbor of Brest—for it is France still!—see that gigantic cable plunging with the noise of thunder, with the swiftness of lightning! It sinks into the waves, dispelling, as it goes, the monsters of the deep, and braving the stress of storms. It stretches from Europe to America, to carry messages, not of war but of peace, and to fix as a reality the union of the three nations which form the aristocracy of the world, and which, whenever they shall so choose, have power to establish throughout our planet the reign of peace—America, England, and France! [*Enthusiastic applause.*]

III. The Virtues. Ladies and Gentlemen, human society rests on a deeper and more sacred basis than mere interests, or even ideas. The moral order is the necessary foundation of the social order. It would be an illusion, then, to suppose that the various forces just enumerated are sufficient of themselves to maintain peace, and that they may safely cut loose from this supreme force—virtue. Our honorable and learned Chairman has just exhibited the disordered passions of the heart as a permanent principle of war. Permit me to remark that I had said this very thing on the subject of *war* in a lecture of mine, for which some of the friends of peace have complained of me. I said "war is the ideal of sin, the ideal of the brute and the devil." [*Applause.*] But it is just because it is the ideal of the brute and the devil, that it is, in one aspect, the ideal of man. There is something of the brute and of the devil in man. The root of war is in pride, concupiscence, revenge—in all the bad passions that ferment within us. It is our burden and our glory to struggle against these; but if we would conquer them, we must not ignore their existence and energy. To banish war, to say to it what the Lord says to death—" O death, I will be thy death"—we must make exterminating war on sin—sin of society as well as of the individual—sin of peoples as well as of kings. We must record and expound to the world, which does not understand them as yet, those two great books of public and private morality, the book of the synagogue, written by Moses with the fires of Sinai, and transmitted by the prophets to the Christian Church; and our own book, the book of grace, which upholds and fulfils the law, the gospel of the Son of God. The decalogue of Moses, and the gospel of Jesus Christ! The decalogue which speaks of righteousness, while showing at the height of righteousness the fruit of charity; the gospel which speaks of charity, while showing in the roots of charity the sap of righteousness. This is what we need to affirm by word and by example, what we need to glorify before peoples and kings alike! [*Prolonged applause.*]

Thank you for this applause! It comes from your hearts, and it is intended for these divine books! In the name of these two books, I accept it. I accept it also in the name of those sincere men who group themselves about these books, in Europe and America. It is a most palpable fact that there is no room in the daylight of the civilized world except for these three religious communions, Catholicism, Protestantism, and Judaism! [*Renewed applause.*]

The want of a peace catechism has been spoken of with regret. We have one. Something more detailed in form, or more appropriate to our special wants, may be desirable, but I must assert that the catechism is already made. You need but carry the decalogue to its conclusions. You need but apply to nations the principles of individual morality, and abolish that refuge of lies—one rule for private life, and another for public life. [*Good! good!*]

"Thou shalt not kill," says the everlasting law. But does it only condemn the cowardly and cruel wretch who skulks behind his victim and plunges a dagger into his heart, or blows out his brains with a pistol? Is murder no longer a crime when it is committed on a great scale, and is the act of a prince or of a deliberative assembly? What! think you that without breaking God's law, without offending human conscience, without branding on your forehead the mark of Cain, without heaping burning coals on your head—think you that you can lay open to the gaze of history those vast fields of carnage, and there, for the gratification of your whim or the accomplishment of your design, mow down your fellow-creatures with grape-shot by the hundred-thousand? Cain! Cain where is Abel thy brother? [*General applause.*]

"Thou shalt not kill," says the law. It also says, "Thou shalt not steal." Here is a poor man. His wife and children, emaciated with want, are languishing on foul straw in one of those penfolds that abound in great cities filled with luxurious palaces. In the fever of his distress, in the delirium excited in his soul by the tears he has supped from his wife's cheeks and his little children's hands, this man snatches a loaf of bread, or a piece of money, and brings back, not joy, but life into the dwelling of famine. Thither human justice pursues him; it tears him from that weeping family; it smites him, with one blow, in his love, his honor, and his liberty. And here, on the other hand, is a government which is meditating some straightening or other of the frontier without—[*applause*]—some able diversion of public attention within—[*applause*]—some trap or other, baited with glory to catch liberty—[*shouts of Bravo, long continued;*]—and while waiting for the judgment of history, and the surer judgment of God, the public conscience will condone, perhaps will glorify, the robbery of so many cities or provinces, the crafty or violent annexation of a whole people! For my part, as a minister of the living God, laying my hand upon the Ten Commandments, I am not afraid to say: In the former case, if there be sin, it is venial sin; in the latter case it is mortal sin! [*Long applause.*]

"Thou shalt not covet," proceeds the book of inspiration. And in fact, in the judgment of the Christian conscience, the sin is not only in the hand that acts, it is in the longing eye, the plotting heart. O kings, potentates, peoples—for the peoples have their times of madness, and democracies as well as personal governments, have those who flatter them to their ruin—[*applause*]—whoever you are, kings or peoples, ye shall not covet! Ye shall not say, We bide our time; and as the brigand bides his, in the darkness of his den, ye shall not sniff in advance the savor of the blood ye do not dare to shed. Ye shall not covet.

You see, Ladies and Gentlemen, what is wanted is not to construct a catechism, it is to reconstruct history. We do not want to be taught henceforth from the cradle upward that the greatest glory is that of the conqueror. [*Applause.*] What you must tell your children—I speak to you, mothers—is that the man who makes two blades of grass grow where one grew before, has done more for mankind than the victor of twenty battles; that they should respect the independence of nations as they respect the modesty of women; that it is as cowardly and criminal to insult the independence of a neighboring country as to tolerate insults on the independence of our own. [*Renewed applause.*]

Ah! if it were a war of independence, I would be the first, if not to wage it, at least to preach it. If the flag of France were at the frontier for defence and not for attack, torn it might be by bullets, blackened with smoke, red with blood, but around it we would rally, one and all, and it would not waver! Dear, glorious flag! if warriors' hands were lacking, the hands of our women would grasp the staff, and it would not waver. [*Good! good!*]

I have spoken of justice; but justice alone is not enough, whether between nations or between individuals. There must be charity with it. Why is it that the law is so hard, so impossible to keep, until the Spirit of grace descends into the heart? It is because mere justice is an irksome thing. It limits our rights by the rights of others, and restricts the sphere of our activity. But let love enter the heart and expand it until it finds its own good and its own happiness in the happiness and good of others, and the law is no longer hard to keep. It becomes a necessity of the soul as well as a duty. This is the meaning of that deep saying of St. Augustine, "only love, and you may do what you choose." But to this end, the nations, not satisfied with being just, must be good, kind, trustful toward each other. The nations of Europe must maintain among themselves dispositions like those of provinces of the same country.

Does the prosperity of one of our provinces produce invidious feelings in the rest? No; because in their individuality—too imperfect, in my opinion, but real, nevertheless—they form the grand unit, France. Well, let each of the nations of the continent consider itself a province of that United States of Europe, which has not yet received its political constitution, but has received its moral one. Then, in the superior unity which knits together their interests, and instead of impairing, strengthens and develops them, they will learn to trust each other; and when, as the result of honorable effort—of industry and virtue—the prosperity of one of them shall be increased, it will not excite fear in any quarter, but pride and satisfaction everywhere. The little States will say, We have one protector more. And the great States will open ranks to welcome a new and potent auxiliary.

But how much closer and holier this unity becomes, when we consider it in its relations to Christianity! I have referred already to the wonderful teaching of St. Paul. "The nations are fellow-heirs, and of the same body."* "*Concorporales:*" it is one of those new words coined by Christianity to express the new ideas which it

* Ephesians, iii. 6.

brought into the world, the idea of true cosmopolitanism and humanitarianism, the idea of the city and people of God! The nations are more than consolidated; they are *concorporeal*, because they are "partakers of one promise," and of one divine life, "in Christ by the gospel."

Ladies and Gentlemen, I call to mind the first appearance of the symbol of the cross on a military standard. A prince, of whom I speak reservedly—for though in certain relations he was the benefactor of the gospel, he also, in my opinion, inflicted on it no little injury—Constantine the Great—[*tokens of approval*]—at that moment he was great, indeed, for he was struggling against the blind and violent resistance of expiring paganism; in one of those prophetic dreams which come to great men on the eve of the great events of their lives and of the world's life, Constantine saw the Christ holding in his hands, oh wonder! a flag of war; but on that flag was traced the cross!

The cross upon the flag! It is first the transformation of war, and then its destruction: transformation by justice and charity, destruction by peace. No! since that ray of heaven marked out the cross upon the Labarum, there must be no war save just war, waged only for the defence of right against violent aggression, and consequently against war, and in the interest of peace. All other war than this is pagan, even though Christians be its soldiers; and the cross of Jesus which it profanes shall be avenged, in the judgment of the last day. No! under the standard of the cross, no more of hatred, revenge, cruelty! But on these fields of horror, yet of moral beauty, the same hands which have inflicted wounds shall come near, trembling with pity, I had almost said with remorse, to stanch and heal. Instead of that savage war-cry of antiquity, *Væ victis*, "woe to the vanquished!"—there shall be seen and heard nothing but love toward the conquered, and respect.

The day shall come, it may be ages from this time—but to the thought of God, and to the life of humanity, ages are but days—when the light of the cross shall shine out upon the prophetic Labarum, and the battle-standard shall be thenceforth only the standard of the immortal victory of peace.

In the present age of the world, universal and perpetual peace is only a chimera. In the age to come, it will be a reality. For my part, I have always believed—and now, in this assembly of my brethren, I don't mind telling the secret—I have always believed that in some nearer or remoter future, mankind would come, not to complete perfection, which does not belong to earth, but to that relative perfection which precedes and prepares for heaven. After the fall of Jerusalem and Rome, and the predicted end of the ancient world, the primitive Christians, heirs of the promises of Jewish prophecy, did not expect immediately the beginning of the heavenly and eternal state, but a temporal reign of Jesus Christ and his saints, a regeneration and triumph of man upon the earth. I, also, look for this mysterious millennium, about which our errors of detail cannot shake the deep, unalterable truth. I look for it, and in the humble but faithful measure of my labors, my words, my prayers, I strive to prepare the way for it. I believe that nations as well as individuals shall some day taste the fruit of universal redemption by the Son of God made man. I believe that the law and the gospel shall reign over this whole planet. I believe that we—that you and I—shall see descending from heaven a manhood humbler and nobler, meeker and mightier, purer and more loving, in a word, grander, than our own. "And this man shall be the peace!" *Et erit iste Pax.**

Over the cradle of our Lord Jesus Christ the angels sung, in the majestic beauty of that Christmas night, "Glory to God in the highest, and on earth peace, good-will to men." And over the tomb from which he rose, the cradle of his new life, Christ says himself, "I have overcome the world! My peace I give to you!" The future shall receive that promise of the angels, and that gift of Christ—the double hosanna of his cradle and his tomb. The future is the inheritance, not of the violent, but of the meek. Then shall be brought to pass that other saying, written among the words that shall never pass away, "Blessed are the meek, for they shall inherit the earth." [*Loud and long-continued applause.*]

* Micah, v. 5.

THE NOTRE-DAME LECTURES.
ADVENT, 1867.

CIVIL SOCIETY IN ITS RELATIONS WITH CHRISTIANITY.

LECTURE FIRST.
December 1, 1867.

CIVIL SOCIETY IN ITS RELATIONS WITH DOMESTIC SOCIETY.

MY LORD ARCHBISHOP AND GENTLEMEN: In entering, last year, upon the study of social questions in their moral and religious aspect, we distinguished, at the outset, three principal forms of society, which, for different but equally imperative reasons, are essential to the perfect organization of mankind on the earth: domestic society, or the family—civil society, or the State; religious society, or the Church. We have spoken of the family. The subject needed years—we devoted to it six lectures; but as far as our limits allowed us we have treated of that subject.

The order of subjects brings me, this year, to the consideration of Civil Society, or the State.

But is this a time for bringing such a subject into the Christian pulpit? Is it becoming to lift up a voice

—a priest's voice, which should be ever grave and calm—amid the tumult of heated passions, and, so to speak, under the gleam of the lightning and the roll of thunder? This, Gentlemen, is the very thing which attracts me. Not that I love danger. I remember the word of our holy Book: "He who seeks peril shall perish in it himself."* I do not love danger, but I go through it without fear when it lies between me and duty. Yes, it is a duty for the minister of the gospel, at least in this presence; the hour is solemn and propitious; and because the men of error and the men of hate have been speaking too loud, and because events have given echo to their voice, it is full time to lift up, above, far above the clamor of parties, the impartial voice of righteousness and truth.

And then, Gentlemen, what reassures me is your presence—the presence of this audience, the very sight of which imposes on me wisdom and moderation—the presence of the eminent prelate whose benediction I have just received. To tell you my inmost thought, I am reassured by my own conscience. A loyal, respectful subject of the Government of my country, firmly resolved to follow no political flag save that which may rally about it all honest citizens, the flag of the legitimate elevation, the material, and still more the moral elevation, of the most numerous and the most suffering classes of society. If I look deeper in my heart, I find, it is true, two passions; but I am not afraid freely to avow them in your presence. The first is the passion —the burning passion—of love for the holy catholic, apostolic, and Roman Church, our mother, the mother of Europe and America, the mother of the great civilization of the West. And then, beside her, with her,

* Ecclesiasticus, iii. 27.

within her, the passion of love to France, which has always been, and shall ever be her eldest daughter.

I am not, then, out of my place in discussing social questions in their relations with the gospel, with morality and religion. I am in my place, because I am a priest, and because I am a citizen; because I have not abdicated for the heavenly country the interests and the love of my earthly country; because, my Lord Archbishop, I remember that what has been the motto of your whole life, has been in recent days one of your most eloquent inspirations at St. Genevieve, at that festival which I might call the wedding of science and faith, when you saluted, in the name both of the one and of the other, "those two things which ought to control the whole of human life—country and religion."

PART FIRST.—*The Origin and End of Civil Society in its Relation to Domestic Society.*

[Having to *define* Civil Society in this first Lecture, Father Hyacinthe considered that he could not better do this than by comparing it with Domestic Society, which precedes it in the world both in the order of history and in the order of reason, and is consequently a natural limit to its rights. He would treat, then, successively, of the origin and end of Civil Society in its relation to the Family.]

I. At the outset, I find myself face to face with an immense error bequeathed to us by the ancients, by the philosophy and jurisprudence of Greece and Rome. It consists in confounding the social order in general, which is essential to the existence of mankind on the earth, with civil society, which is only a particular form of the social order; and, coming nearer to our present subject, it supposes that the family did not exist before the commonwealth; that it received from civil society its constitution, its laws, and its spirit; that consequently civil society possesses over the family, over its internal affairs, and over its substantial rights, a power, so to speak, unlimited.

You see that we are concerned at the very start with a question of origin between the two societies which we are comparing. Which of the two comes first? Historically and logically, in the order of ideas and in the order of facts, which is the root and which the fruit?

Against the authority of the pseudo-philosophers of the eighteenth century, and of the pseudo-politicians of the French Revolution, I declare that civil society is relatively of recent date, and that domestic society preceded it, I do not say by years, but by ages.

I ask the Bible. I have told you before, I am not ashamed of the Bible. Anti-religious prejudice may deny its inspiration; but it cannot contest its historical authority. I take the Bible, which one of the deepest thinkers of our age has called "the book of humanity," the Bible, which is not the history of a political organization or of a religious sect, but the history of the great race of man; I open its first book, the book of the beginning, Genesis. Nothing, here, of empire or republic, nothing about political society, but from end to end it breathes the pure and fruitful spirit of domestic society! From the marriage-bed of Adam and Eve, to the wandering tents of Abraham, Isaac, and Jacob—everywhere domestic society!

But this page of ancient Scripture, how it is displayed before our eyes, subjected to our very touch, in contemporary facts! Providence is wonderful in its inventions. It has written the history of our globe and its primeval transformations in the bowels of the earth, and day by day, as these are laid open, geologists bring up again before our eyes the unknown ages unmeasured by the life of man. But it has been not less ingenious for the moral world; only, instead of dumb relics entombed in death, it reveals to us living relics which it has cherished in the bosom of the human family, in such wise that the successive stages which our race has passed through, are displayed to us simultaneously in the light of day.—I transport myself with you for a moment to those lofty summits of the globe, those table-lands of central Asia which have been so well styled "the hive of nations." It is the region of heavy grasses, and from immemorial time the dwelling-place of nomadic tribes. It is one of the most magnificent and fascinating sights which man can contemplate. Nothing equals the *steppe*, or at least nothing surpasses it; not the sea with its monotonous and majestic immensity, nor the virgin forest with its mysterious depths, nor the mountains with their sublime upspringing of earth toward heaven. Plains without end, covered in spring with luxuriant and spontaneous vegetation; an ocean of flowers and verdure, undulating from east to west, from west to east, under the June breezes; towering grasses, the offspring of nature, untouched by the sweat of man's brow, engulfing in their dense growth the caravans of the desert, men, horses, camels, even, and spreading afar their intoxicating perfumes! . . . . For whom has God made these favored regions? Was it for those savages who, according to Rousseau and the "*Contrat Social*," everywhere preceded the establishment of civil society? Was it for that man-monkey which the false science of our generation exhibits to us, struggling through ages of endeavor to free itself from the limitations of brute-existence? "For my part," remarked an eminent traveller to me, on his return from these distant lands, "what I saw over there was a great deal of Abraham!" And in fact, excepting the purity of the primitive religion, which has decayed among them, it is a marvellous relic of that patriarchal society the simplicity of which is so superior, in grandeur and beauty, to the complicated and scientific organization of our civil society. These are the nomadic shepherds among whom intercourse with nature has developed a remarkable practical sense and meditative intelligence; these are the communities sustained only by tradition and the domestic virtues, among which each father of a family commands in authority and in liberty .... Hail, sacred deserts, plains of Tartary, that have poured out again and again your healing floods eastward toward China—westward toward Greece and Russia; peradventure for us also ye are guarding the secret of the future! Ah! if we continue to slip along this fatal slope, if we go on in the progress of decay to atheism in doctrine, to materialism in morals, to revolt against all authority worthy of the name, to servitude under every revolutionary despotism; if our posterity follows us into these lower depths—O then, ye plains of Tartary, send forth to us our latest saviors! Trample us beneath the hoofs of your steeds; smite us down with the weapons of your warriors, and then, baptized with the lingering remains of our Christianity, rise up like the Germans and the Huns of yore, and you will have snatched Europe from the corruption in which it has been dragged by sophists and harlots, by demagogues and tyrants!

[After having established by the Bible, by history, and by contemporary geography, the priority of domestic society to civil society, Father Hyacinthe proved that on the contrary it is the State which has its origin and the ground of its existence in the necessities of the family. As he has already observed, he means here by *State* not merely the sovereign power of civil society, but the whole nation in so far as it constitutes such society. In opposition to the error of the "social compact" which represents civil society as an arbitrary work of man, there comes up the error of certain philosophers and theologians who regard it as being directly and exceptionally a divine creation. This error originates in confounding the *supernatural* organization of the polity of the Hebrews, and the *natural* organization of the polity of other nations. It is an error which predisposes the State to put itself in the place which belongs of right to the family, and to extend the exercise of its supremacy to private life.]

I acknowledge, Gentlemen, that many of our philosophers and theologians have not kept quite clear of this doctrine. Must it be confessed?—Bossuet is one of them. I own no connection with that line of vulgar detractors who think to magnify themselves by attacking Bossuet. Bossuet, the last link in the august tradition of the Fathers of the Church! Bossuet, the glory, not of France, but of all catholicism! But the loftiest genius is affected in some degree by the delusive spirit of its age. Bossuet came after the ruin of those Middle Ages, which, misunderstand them as we may, were in so many respects an era of liberty. He lived in the splendor of those absolute monarchies which have risen upon the modern world, and which seem to have concentred the whole social system in themselves. Under the dominion of the prejudices of his time, it was possible for this great man to teach that the right of property was derived from the Government, and that "in general every right must needs be derived from the public authority."* But pushed to its last results, and aimed, in turn, by the absolutism of demagogues against the absolutism of

---

* Politique tirée des propres paroles de l'Ecriture Sainte, livre Ier, Art. iii., propos. iv.

kings, such a principle would justify the crimes of the French Revolution, and the criminal dreams of socialism itself.

No; the right of property is not derived from the State! Land, that foothold of the family, that basis of the home, is owned by a better title than the concession of the State! It takes hold of the deepest secrets of human nature, the most absolute necessities of a free and intelligent man. The Columbus of primitive ages, or of newly discovered regions, I tread some uninhabited land. I gaze upon it in its virgin beauty,—its wild uncomeliness, perhaps;—no matter, I am charmed by it. I form with it that bond, so full of mystery, which unites person and thing, and in which interest, reason, affection itself, are intertwisted. Ah! when I have done this, there is no power on earth, even though it call itself Louis XIV., which has the right to stand up and say, as this monarch once said, "I am the owner, you are the tenant." No! the owner is myself. It is all mine, soil as well as crop. You cannot rend that patch of earth from me; neither can you give me a title to it. My right consists in the act of my will, which said to this field, this forest, "Be mine." My right consists in the landmark I have placed, in the hedge I have planted. My right! it is in the sweat of my brow, the blood upon my hands, the rude embraces with which my love and labor have seized and fertilized the land. Henceforth that land belongs to the person of man. I hold it in my own right, and God stands by me in the claim.

[Doubtless when the existence of a central and sovereign power is necessary to the maintenance of justice and peace between domestic communities hitherto independent of each other, this power is ordained of God; "for there is no power but of

God;"* and it is not free to the several heads of families to refuse their assent to the institution of it. But this institution is not effected directly by God. Only one such instance is furnished by history;—the Jewish nation, well styled the miraculous nation. This nation was formed by God, at Sinai; but the nation was itself the Church of Jesus Christ in a preparative stage. The historical origin of civil society has considerably varied in different times and places, with different races and in different circumstances; but the underlying reason which has produced and maintained it, is the need felt by families of a new organization to regulate and protect their rights. This takes place often in consequence of the change from the wandering pastoral life to the settled life of the husbandman. Abraham and Lot, nomadic shepherds, may separate from each other on the face of the earth: the tribes descended from Jacob, and planted on the soil by Joshua, need, if they would dwell in peace, judges, and by and by kings. War, also, was a potent means of organization for political society: blood is the primitive cement of the most of them, and the earliest kings were soldiers that had been crowned by victory. Sometimes it is the defender of a group of families against outside aggressions who, victorious, becomes the organizer of society; sometimes it is the enemy himself who becomes first conqueror, then legislator.]

II. But whatever the facts may have been with regard to the historical origin of civil society, we have now reached the philosophical notion of it. It is the union of a certain number of heads of families, in order that the mutual exercise of their rights may be regulated by common arbitrament, and, if necessary, protected by force. This union supposes an agreement, implied if not expressed, between the heads of families, which bears no resemblance to the "social compact," since it is ordained by Providence, demanded, at a certain stage of development, by human nature, and governed by the absolute principles of justice.

* Romans, xiii. 1.

Look on the brow of the father, on the gray hair of the patriarch. It is encircled by a triple crown, the tiara, if I might call it so, of secular authority. When I behold the pontiff of the Catholic Church, the father of redeemed humanity—let me call him by his name, that sweet name that grows in glory as it grows in experience of trial—when I behold Pius IX., I see upon his gentle and majestic brow three crowns not to be disjoined. In primeval times, when as yet there was no universal pope, these three crowns were worn by the pontiff of every dwelling: he was father, king, and priest. Oh, how lovely, and at the same time how venerable, the father's crown! I salute it with trembling lips. Thou art a father, O aged patriarch with hoary head, that gatherest upon thy knees and in thy bosom the children of three generations! Thou art a father, O son of man, that hast reached the highest grade of natural greatness possible to humanity; from thy loins have sprung a numerous seed, in thy heart have been treasured all the affections of humanity, on thy voice waits obedience only less complete than that which is yielded to God. A father, thou art a priest as well. Thus far, Christ has not yet come into the world with his sacerdotal institution, with his bishops and priests; thou standest alone in the sanctuary of the household, holding all their consciences in thy hand, uniting all their prayers in thy prayer, offering all their hearts in thy heart. A priest, thou art a king withal! Thou stretchest forth the sceptre of righteousness to regulate and guard all rights; thou bearest the sword to defend and to avenge, as Abraham, a mere head of family, using the right of war which belonged to him, rescued his nephew's family from the hands of his enemies. . . .

Now, from the head of the father of the family

these two crowns, of priest and of king, have fallen off. The priestly crown has passed, in part at least, in the constitution of religious society, to the Catholic hierarchy. The royal diadem has passed altogether, in the organization of civil society, to the chiefs of the State. To civil society, whatever the form of it, republic or empire, belong now the sceptre and the sword. But the father of the family still retains all his rights, excepting that one which consists in regulating and guarding all the rest, and which constitutes the sovereign power.

One of the acutest and exactest thinkers of our day, whom I desire to mention by name on account of the obligation I am under to him in my own studies, the illustrious Abbé Rosmini-Serbati—a genuine Italian to the very marrow of his bones, and at the same time a Catholic to the very core of his heart—has helped me to the best conception of civil society. According to him, civil society has for its object, not, like the family in the natural order, or the Church in the supernatural order, the *substance* of rights, but simply the *modality* of rights. It does not create rights. Man exists before the State, with all those essential and inalienable rights which he holds directly from God, by virtue of reason and moral liberty. The family, also, exists before the State, with rights equally essential, equally inalienable, exercised in its bosom by the human person raised to his fullest dignity and felicity. It is not for the State to create those rights which are antecedent to it, and which come, I am bold to say, from a far higher source; it is only for the State not to destroy them nor encroach upon them. Its mission extends no further than to protect them, and to establish over them the sway of what the English, in their noble language, call "the queen's peace"—what Saint Paul bids us ask for when we pray for kings and all that are in authority, "that we may lead a quiet and peaceable life in all godliness and honesty."* The mission of the State consists, then, in fixing the *modality* of rights, that is, in regulating the best way in which the reciprocal duties of individuals and families should be exercised in order to help rather than hinder each other in their common development. It consists, further, in protecting by force the rights and interests which belong to it from every unjust and violent attack, whether from within or from without. Such are the natural frontiers of civil society and domestic society, the family and the State—frontiers far more important for the peace and liberty of the world than those of the Pyrenees, the Alps, or the Rhine!

On these frontiers I pause, and salute that sceptre which requires nothing but righteousness, produces nothing but peace; the oppressor of none, the liberator of all. I salute the sword of which Saint Paul declares that the king bears it not in vain.† Next to righteousness, I know nothing more sacred than force, when force is not the assassin of right, but its champion.

PART SECOND.—*The Mutual Rights of Domestic Society and of Civil Society in Relation to the Marriage Contract, to Education, and to the Sanctity of Wills.*

[In this second part, Father Hyacinthe proposes to consider the three principal functions of domestic life, in their relation to civil society. Birth, love, death, are the three crises of individual life; and transposing these terms according to the social order of the family, of which love is the basis, we have the contract of husband and wife, the education of children, the testament of the aged.

---

* 1 Timothy, ii. 2. † Romans, xiii. 4.

1. *The Marriage Contract.*—Father Hyacinthe gave notice that he did not intend, at this time, to consider the marriage contract in its specifically Christian aspect, and in the supernatural order, in which it is exalted to the dignity of a sacrament; that he treated of it here in a more general way, and wherever it exists, as the fundamental act of domestic society. He sets the State, then, in comparison, not with the Church, but with the family.

After remarking that the State invades the domain of individual liberty when it imposes marriage, as Augustus did in a famous law, or when it interdicts it, like certain States of modern Germany, the orator comes directly on the question of the power of the State over the contract considered in itself. This power does not affect the substance of the contract, but only the civil solemnities which accompany it, the civil effects which follow it, and on which it belongs to the civil power to determine; it is the modality of right. There is, then, no propriety in the expression, sometimes used, of "civil marriage," and Pope Pius VI. was right when he declared in a brief that "marriage is a natural contract, instituted and confirmed antecedently to all civil society." So that it is not only the sanctity of the sacrament which the Church has in every age so energetically defended against the attacks of secular powers; it is more than this, it is the integrity of the rights of the family.]

For this cause I bless thee, O my Church! Church Catholic, Church of the Middle Ages, and of the great pontiffs, Gregory VII. and Innocent III.! Not alone for the sanctity of thy sacrament hast thou contended, thou hast been the defender of the liberty of our consciences, the purity of our morals, the peace and dignity of our homes.... The Church has defended the family; and because the soul of the family is, so to speak, concentrated in the wife, a priceless treasure in a frail vessel, it is especially over woman that it extends its protection;—woman, with whom the Church has affinities so affecting and sublime, that it were vain to attempt to sunder them; woman, whose liberty is always appealed to when the design is to oppress or to corrupt her: the Church defended her against the violence of the powerful in days of yore, as it now defends her against the barbarity of sophists. It covers her with the shield of its wrath, which the prophets so well speak of* as "the fury of the dove" and "the wrath of the Lamb," and stretching over her its unarmed, but terrible hand, it tells the monarch, quailing before it in his pride and lust,

"This woman is God's charge; forbear thy hand."

[2. *The Education of Children.*—Father Hyacinthe alluded to his argument of last year's lecture, showing how education, being the complement or rather the chief element of parental authority, the care of it belongs, of natural right, to the parents. The State, doubtless, has the right to keep watch over instruction, and to hinder anything from entering into it detrimental to public morality and peace; but it may not impose on families a system of education, nor enforce the employment of such and such a school or teacher.]

The child belongs to its parents. I know the prejudices of my contemporaries; but I affirm none the less, in some measure, a right of property of man in man; and there can be no example of this sort of right more legitimate and noble than that of the right of the father to the child. Doubtless the *person* of every human being is essentially free and sovereign; it belongs to itself, under the "eminent domain" of God. But it is not so with its *nature*. Saving and excepting the rights of the person, we may say—we *must* say—that the nature of the son belongs to the father. It is flesh of his flesh and bone of his bone. The breath which inspires it is breathed from his nostrils. The vital heat which ani-

---

* Jeremiah, xxv. 38 (Vulgate, "*a facie iræ columbæ.*") Revelation, vi. 16.

mates it is kindled from himself; and as they were wont to say in Israel, it is his spark, his lamp, which is to go shining on when he is dead, and perpetuate his name and glory in the midst of his people. The father is then, indeed, the proprietor of this sacred nature; to him alone it belongs to impress upon it its controlling momentum and direction toward the future. Consequently the school, the sanctuary of education, has its proper place beneath or near the parental roof.

We are proud of France, and with good reason; but it is not right for us to despise other countries. There are countries of Europe which are of value to us in many relations, and may well serve us as models. Let me cite a touching example of primary instruction as it is given at the family fireside in certain parts of Norway. In those mountainous regions, so sombre and sad in their gentle beauty, but so rugged in climate during the cold season, the summer is devoted to the culture of the fields, the winter to the household. It gathers, then, about the fireside, the radiant centre of light and heat both for body and for soul, and there the education of the children is taken in hand. The most aged of the family overlook the task; the mother and the elder sisters are the teachers, aided, commonly, by the travelling schoolmaster, a household pilgrim, whose business takes him about through the snow-paths, with his little baggage of Christian science and national history and poetry. Beside the schoolmaster, and sometimes in his vacant chair, sits the minister of religion—a Protestant minister, I know, but ordinarily a man who has kept the vital principle of Christianity, with the faith of Christ and the morality of the gospel. At this house-school is forming, day by day, the character of generations in whom the religious and patriotic sentiments are far stronger and more closely united than with us.

[It is not, however, the rule that the school is kept in the family; but if it is detached from the fireside, it should nevertheless not cease to be dependent on it. It is by the law of nature that the schoolmaster is subordinate to the parent. He is the auxiliary, not the rival of the father and mother; he is to carry forward their work, not destroy it.]

The public interest, that pagan idea so often appealed to against the rights of the individual and the family, could not give to the State a power over education which it does not possess itself. In Sparta, the republic claimed the right of educating the children, because it regarded them as its property; and this principle was, in a greater or less degree, that of all Greek and Roman antiquity.* This is what the latest type of democracy seems ready to reproduce amongst us. It puts at the head of its programme, Obligatory Instruction—obligatory, not only as to the fact of instruction (which of itself would be too much), but as to the school and as to the teachers. We can have no doubt of what its design is, in view of its systematic enmity to the liberty of teaching in general, and to religious instruction in particular. It means to deliver future generations from the influences of the family, which form the chief hindrance to its plans, and to its so-called "progress." It means to supplant the customary mould of domestic education with the mighty mould of national education; to withdraw the school from the family, in order to give it over to the exclusive control of the State.

* The grand principle of Lycurgus, repeated in express terms by Aristotle, was that as the children belong to the State, they should be educated by the State, according to the views of the State. (See Rollin's Ancient History.)

Such is the liberty which they have in preparation for us! Such is their boasted democracy! And with such a platform as this they dare to make their appeal to universal suffrage. Ah! I have a respect for the ballot-box of France, but I have a higher respect for its home. Leave its ballot-boxes free, and leave its households sovereign! True national education is the free and harmonious resultant of all the educations of the household. True public opinion is the great soul of a people breathing at once from every fireside. However mighty, however enlightened the Government of any nation, it has neither the mission nor the right to fashion that nation in its own image and likeness, and to run it in the mould which it has wrought. It has simply to receive the nation such as it has grown of itself, such as it has come down to it with each of its generations growing up in the bosom of the family, such as it has been moulded in the minds of fathers, in the hearts of mothers, in the discipline of teachers chosen by father and mother, private teachers or public, lay or clerical—no matter what, so long as they are the choice of the parents, and therefore representatives of the family and of Christianity.

[3. *The Right of Bequest.*—The supreme act of parental authority and providence is not education, but testation. The right of testation, one of the sublimest rights that can be exercised by a human being, is sublimer yet when it is vested in the person of the father. In every man, it is a grand affirmation of *the immortality of the soul.* In the case of the father, it affirms, besides, the principle of *the immortality of the family,* and, by a sequence too little understood, the principle of *the immortality of the nation.* Here, too, civil society is under obligation to regulate the forms and guard the effects of this act; but it cannot tamper with the right itself, nor rob the father of the family of the liberty of testation.]

The greatest philosopher of Germany, great in heart as well as in genius, Leibnitz, saw in the Will a supreme affirmation of *the immortality of the soul.* The Will, in fact, is not a contract, or, to use the barbarous expression of some writers, a "quasi-contract" between one living man and others. It is the Will of the dead. "A testament," says St. Paul, and all legislation agrees with him, "a testament is of force after men are dead; otherwise it is of no strength at all while the testator liveth."* It is in the Will that the ancestor, if I may so speak, rises in his grave, wiser and more potent in death than in life, marks out to his posterity the course that they must follow, and proclaims the law of the future. It is in vain that men assert that all rights perish with the present life. The testament is the will of the dead imposing duties on the living. It is, I will not say a *moral* relation, that is too weak a word, it is a *juridical* relation formed from the two sides of the tomb, and constituting one of the bonds of that universal society which Leibnitz called *the commonwealth of souls.* It is no chimera, thou sage of Germany, this commonwealth of souls. It is a truth, and we are coming back to it.

How then could Robespierre, that great foe of the family and of the Will, put the question before the Constituent Assembly, which refused to listen (the Convention did listen to it at a later day)—how could he put the question: "Is a man to be allowed to dispose of the land he cultivated, after he himself has gone to dust?" No, Robespierre, you were wrong, you gave the lie to your own nobler instincts. Was it not yourself, some years later, who, at the sight of the revolutionary atheism that was swelling from that time and now overflows upon us, affrighted at the fruit of your loins, O

* Hebrews, ix. 17.

grand though sanguinary tribune—was it not yourself who invoked God and the immortal soul of man as the last salvation of the people in its madness?

[The liberty of testation in the father of the family is also the effective principle of *the immortality of the family.*]

The family is not a structure reared for a few years at most, built on the marriage contract, and taken down when the children come of age. It is an institution which passes down the ages, like the State itself, of which it is the more lasting basis. In a learned and eloquent plea for the wise enlargement of the liberty of testation, an eminent magistrate, who now occupies a seat in the council of his sovereign, exhibits to us the picture of this institution, parcelled out in its patrimony, enfeebled in its authority, and arrived at a point of degradation which compromises it as a power in society.* The mortal wound dealt to the family by Robespierre and the Convention, has been but imperfectly healed by the genius of the First Consul. The only effectual remedy is to restore to the hands of the father the plenary power needful for the repression of evil and the encouragement of good in the society which he governs. On the son who has dishonored his name and corrupted his blood by vice, paternal justice, full of mercy, must be able to inflict punishment salutary to all, recovering, perhaps, the guilty, protecting from him the rest of the family. To the family itself he must be able to bequeath the elements of prosperity and continuance, which at present are sorely lacking.

Between the family and the land which supports and sustains it, there grow up ties which ought not to be

* Speech on the right of Testation in its Relations with Paternal Authority, by M. Pinard, procurer-general. Page 58.

broken with every generation: the family homestead is a Holy Land, like that which God promised to the seed of the patriarchs; and the hearth, the central point of it, has all the dignity of its Most Holy Place. Shall this homestead be parcelled out in patches? The works which grow up with it, in agriculture or other industries, shall they come to naught? Shall the fireside be given over to strangers? Shall these articles of household use, redolent of the remembrances of former kindred, be sold under the hammer? Ah! Gentlemen, let us show that respect for the domestic hearth with which it is honored by free and virtuous peoples. One such I know, which, like the Hebrew people, has withstood the destructive power of the centuries, and of which a glorious remnant is still left to us. As free under the family roof, as respectful to the public authority, the Basques have written in their *fueros*, on the other side of the Pyrenees, this noble custom: "No public force may approach the house of a Biscayan nearer than nine paces."

* * * * * *

The last of the three great patriarchs, Jacob, was about to die. His eye was dim with age, so that he could not see. But when they told him, "Behold thy sons are coming," the old man gathered up his strength; he kneeled upon his couch, and bowed himself and worshipped at the head of his bed.* Then when he had prayed, renewing his strength by thus waiting on Jehovah, the living and mighty God, he sat upon his bed, his feet resting on the ground, and, taking the best beloved in his arms, he embraced Ephraim and Manasseh

---

* Genesis, xlvii. 31. (Vulgate version, "*Adoravit Israel Deum, conversus ad lectuli caput.*")

before he blessed them. Now mark, Gentlemen, we have here, not the authority of superior age, we have the right of testament! In the experience of his entire life, condensed into that supreme act,—in the prophetic light which shines about him, one feeble ray of which is by and by to glance and touch upon the Christian fathers, Jacob sees the future of each of his children, and takes the measures which the welfare of his race demands. Through the dimness which covers his eyes, with that look of the soul which pierces every veil, he gazes on his eldest son: "Reuben," cries he, "my first-born, that shouldst have been my might, thou hast been the beginning of my troubles. Thou hast flowed away like water. Thou shalt not increase. Thou hast defiled thy father's house, thou canst no longer hold control therein."*

"But thou, Judah, thou art he whom thy brethren shall praise; thy father's children shall bow down before thee. O Judah, how fair thine eyes! They glow like wine within the cup, and whiter are thy teeth than milk. Bind thy foal to the vine, O my son, thine ass's colt to the choice vine. Thou shalt wash thy garments in wine, thy clothes in the blood of the grapes."† How imposing this sight in its simplicity! There they were, twelve men prostrate in tears at the feet of a dying man,—twelve alien Hebrews on the soil of Egypt: and the authority of the father, exercised in the right of testament, consecrated by religious faith, created an immense nation, with whose existence were bound up the destinies of mankind,—an indestructible race, detached at last from its own land under the crush of formidable and repeated invasions, only to fill the whole world with the miracle of its immortality!

* Genesis, xlix. 4. (See the Vulgate version.) † Genesis, xlix. 11, 12.

[In closing, Father Hyacinthe spoke of that *immortality of nations* which has the ground of its existence in the immortality of families.]

The domestic spirit and the national spirit, far from being antagonistic, as the theorizers and jurists of the Revolution conceived, are really developed and strengthened each by the other. A nation is not an assemblage of individuals, but an assemblage of families. A nation of individuals is only the dead body of a nation, buried under the weight of centralized despotism, or galvanized into the convulsions of anarchy. The necessary and providential counterpoise to both despotism and anarchy is found in the family, an element at once conservative and liberal, a principle of order and at the same time of independence.

Let us, then, no longer set up the State in opposition to the family, either on the question of marriage, or on the questions of education and of testament; and since the need of social reforms is felt more keenly at this hour than ever before, let us learn, at last, to understand this great truth, so long misunderstood, that the urgent and decisive reforms are those of domestic life; that political reforms are only of secondary importance.

O statesmen and legislators of my country, turn your attention to questions such as these. They are less fitted, I know, to inflame the passions; but the solution of them would be far more effective for the regeneration of our character, and of the public morals! Ask yourselves what are the means to be employed in order to restore to private life the liberty which it possesses in so inadequate a measure;—to revive in domestic society the spirit of the traditions which used to constitute its vigor! Inquire, above all, by what way and in what measure the authority of the head of the family should be magnified. Cast your eyes, also, upon the frightful ravages which corruption is working among women. . . . Pardon this groan extorted from me by the ignominy of the daughters of my people, the daughters of Israel and of Christian France. . . . . . At our very doors, in England and in Prussia, to say nothing of other countries, there are severe and efficient laws against seduction. Is there nothing for you to do, to guard for our daughters—above all, for the daughters of the common people, for the working-girls in shops and factories—the first, most sacred liberty of all, the liberty of being chaste? The things you censure in the laws, do not approve in books or on the stage. Strive against immorality under every guise which it puts on to work our ruin. Yes! I will not leave this lesson half said! Strive against evil in the bosom of your own family. What! you would be the lawgivers of the nations; you would teach France first, then the West, by what flying leaps the summits of progress and civilization are to be reached! Begin then, lawgivers of the people, by observing the laws of the family, the laws which make husbands virtuous and fathers respected and obeyed. Livy and Seneca speak of the father of the family as a magistrate in his own house—*magistratus domesticus.* Ye household magistrates, check your own passions, control your own homes, and you shall then be worthy of being magistrates of the empire and the commonwealth.

LECTURE SECOND.

DECEMBER 8, 1867.

SOVEREIGNTY.

GENTLEMEN: I approach to-day the question of sovereignty in civil society—a question of peculiar gravity and delicacy. I acknowledge that it is not without misgivings that I set foot on this ground. To be sure, the Catholic Church has given ancient and authoritative instruction in this important department of morals. In every age it has taught the people their duty toward the sovereign, and taught sovereigns their duty toward the people; and I have no novelties of doctrine to introduce here. But am I quite sure, in my weakness, of reproducing the doctrine of the Church with all needful precision and tact? . . . I am encouraged, as heretofore, Gentlemen, by your presence, and by my faith in God. He will give me grace to shun those slippery declivities along which one must encounter irritated passion and political partisanship, and to touch these formidable questions only at the summits which they lift up into that peaceful region which is luminous with thought and duty. In that region, please God, we shall abide together in our study of the subject of political sovereignty.

I set aside, from the start, the famous question of the popular origin of sovereignty. In affirming, as it has often been affirmed in a general way, that the natural and necessary source of all civil authority is in the people, and that consequently there can be no individual or collective person in legitimate possession of power without holding it originally from the nation, it seems to me, to say the least, that the case has been very badly stated. A people is not a people until it is constituted under some sort of government; until then, therefore, it has no political rights. I see a multitude without organization; or rather, I see a congeries of domestic societies in juxtaposition and independence; but I find there no civil society. This is what is perfectly expressed in the ancient maxim: *Tolle unum, turba est; adde unum, populus est.* "Subtract one, it leaves a mob; add one, it makes a nation." The existence of government in civil society is not subsequent to the existence of civil society itself. The two facts are simultaneous and inseparable. Consequently the people cannot be the source of power, since it does not exist as a people except in the presence of power. The Power and the People are twin brothers. Together they come forth from God, the source of all order and all right, and together they return to him.

For the question of the *origin* of sovereignty, I will substitute that of the seat in which sovereignty resides, and I will conclude with that of the *exercise* of sovereignty. This will be more practical, and at the same time more logical and true.

Part First.—*The Seat of Sovereignty.*

[1. The subject wherein sovereignty primarily and absolutely inheres is God himself. In laying down this position Father Hyacinthe merely draws the conclusions which follow from the teachings of the three preceding years, converging on the existence and authority of the personal and living God.]

In that day of utter amazement in which I found myself called to ascend this pulpit, I cried, like Moses,

"Who am I, that I should speak to the children of Israel?"* And from the depth of my heart I heard the answer of God, with that spiritual ear with which every diligent soul, even on earth, may hear it, "Thus shalt thou say unto them, I AM hath sent me unto you."† Thereupon I came to you, in my weakness and in my might, to speak to you of the God of Abraham and Isaac and Jacob—the personal and living God. Before making appeal to revelation I questioned reason, both yours and mine, and from the depth of human thought there came the answer, "I Am that I Am." It was the sovereignty of God in the domain of ideas. The next year we came down together into the lights and shadows of the human conscience, and we sought there the secret of the moral system. The voice of conscience was in unison with the voice of reason. It affirmed the necessary existence of a religious morality and the sovereignty of the God of virtues. Constantly advancing, we entered the first circle of the social system—the family. Here, too, in the authority of the father, in the tenderness and solicitude of the mother, in all the strong and beautiful structure of the household, we recognized the presence of the kingdom of God.

And now, standing face to face with the problems of political philosophy, I have no other answer to give. I speak for myself and for you, and I say, it is God; and again, and always, it is God! The true King as well as the first Father, the supreme Lord of civil as well as of domestic society, is God. He alone is the real Majesty, who covers all their borrowed majesties with the reflection of his glory. "The Lord is our King" .... "yea, the Lord sitteth King forever."‡ From the first page

---

* Exodus, iii. 11.   † Ibid., 14.
‡ Isaiah, xxxiii. 22. Psalms lxxii. 11; xxix. 10.

to the last, the subject-matter of the Bible is the history of his kingdom, and it is summed up by Saint John in the majestic vision of the Apocalypse, in which he beheld the Son of God, the *Logos* of the Father, the everlasting Reason and Righteousness, coming to set up his empire on the earth, sitting on a war-horse, clothed with a vesture dipped in blood, and having on his thigh a name written, *King of kings and Lord of lords.**

But some one will say, this is theocracy.

I am not afraid of a name; and I have already expressed myself on the subject of this one. But since it stirs up about our ears such a storm of hate and malediction, I will return to it. I open the dictionary of the French language, and alongside of it that of the primitive language of Western civilization, the Greek. I look in them for this execrated word, and I find the definition, Power of God. Theocracy, then, is Power derived from God and exercised in God's name. This is that very kingdom of God which I have met from step to step through all my course. In the sovereignty of the idea of Being in the world of ideas, in the sovereignty of the moral law in the world of conscience, in the sovereignty of paternal authority in the home,—everywhere I have come upon theocracy. How could I fail to come upon it in political society? How could it be otherwise, here as elsewhere, but that God should have the sole glory of reigning over man, and man the glory of obeying none but God?

Yes, theocracy! It is no fault of mine if men understand this word in a perverted sense, repugnant at once to etymology and history. It is no fault of ours if we have imputed to us, every day, under this name of theocracy, that notion which we have openly combated and

---

* Revelation, xix. 16.

vanquished—the confusion in the same hands of political and religious power, both of which come from above, but separately and differently. Nowhere in Catholic Christendom do I find this fearful confusion. If you point me to Rome, I do not find there the confusion of these two powers, but the exceptional alliance of them, in a place which is itself exceptional like a miracle. Beneficent alliance! league of the liberty of conscience, never to be untwined, since it unites there what there is need to separate everywhere besides! never has the necessity of it shone more conspicuously than at this hour! Already hast thou received the witness of French blood, shed by those whom men call mercenaries, but who are nothing less than heroes! And now thou art sustained by the truly national eloquence of our orators, and the energetic and loyal declarations of our Government.

[2. After having proved the existence of the theocracy, in that lofty and universal sense in which it is spoken of in the Bible, Father Hyacinthe remarked, that in the political system the sovereignty of God is not exercised immediately and directly. This was done, indeed, among the Israelites, among whom it seemed good to God to preserve for a time, not only the primary right of sovereignty, but also the actual exercise of it. In fulfilling at once the functions of captain, lawgiver, and judge, he marched with the ark at the head of the armies, and gave response from the mercy-seat to political as well as religious questions of conscience. But all this was but a sensible type—we might even say, with Origen, sometimes a gross type—of the sovereignty which he was afterward to exercise over Christian nations by their princes and legislators. " By me kings reign and princes decree justice."* God does not act ordinarily by way of miracle; neither would it be worthy of himself to condescend constantly to the government of States. But those who preside in such government in his name, are only the depositaries of his

---

* Proverbs, viii. 15.

sovereignty, and, as they are called in the holy Book, "the ministers of his kingdom."* It is in this sense that Saint Paul instructs us that "there is no power but of God, that the powers that be are ordained of God."†

Waiving, then, all secondary questions concerning the form of power and the seat of power, Father Hyacinthe remarked only two great facts which have the importance of principles: sovereignty may exist outside of the nation and be exercised over it, or it may exist in the nation and be exercised by it. The first case is that of *an absolute prince;* the second, that *of a sovereign people.*]

1. *The Absolute Prince.*

In considering the origin of society from an abstract point of view, in the order of ideas, I have founded it on a formal or implied compact among the fathers of families—that is, according to the language of the Roman law, among those who are either actually at the head of a family, or who, having come of age, have a right to become such. This is the order of ideas. But the facts of history do not always tally with political metaphysics; and when I come with you to examine the real origin of nations, I find no trace of any such compact. What we most commonly find in place of it, is what has been called "the law of the hero." Instead of nations constituting themselves, I behold mighty and predestinated individuals who create nations, giving birth to them, so to speak, from their own great souls.

The masses, at the beginning, and, it may be, always, need some one's wonder-working finger to be laid upon their breast, in order to call into animation the sleeping spark. Such is a Hercules or a Theseus, slaying monsters, dispersing robbers, by their strength and valor becoming the liberators of oppressed families and the

* Wisdom, vi. 5.   † Romans, xiii. 1.

organizers of nascent society. Such is an Orpheus or an Amphion, towering above the multitude by their wisdom and eloquence—a Numa, commanding them by his piety. From whom do these men receive their power? From the nation? But there is no nation. These are the men who form the nation by the very exercise of power. They reign by force of sword and battle-axe. They rise by virtue of their wisdom and of the benefits they confer. The sovereignty was like the uninhabited land of which I spoke a week ago. God, from the circle of the heaven, humanity from the depth of its wretchedness—everything—was calling for some master, who with one stroke should make it his personal property, and the salvation of all the rest. No vulgar hand might be laid upon it. Make way, then, for the hero! Let him step in to the unoccupied place, be the instrument of righteousness and peace, and, dying, leave the sovereignty to children and children's children, an inalienable and uncontested inheritance!

[This is the power called *absolute*, not because it is absolute in its exercise, since, in this respect, it is subject to the same limitation as popular power, and extends only to the modality of rights, but because it is such in its origin, and its sovereign holds his right of proprietor only from himself and from God. Father Hyacinthe protested against the injustice of the liberal schools of politics, which affect to confound absolute power with arbitrary and despotic power. Absolute power, in the sense in which it has just been explained, is one of the two great forms of sovereignty. It has been the past, it is still the present, of great nations.]

2. *The Sovereign People.*

[The absolutist schools are no less unjust than the liberal schools, when they make *jure-divino* monarchy to be the only legitimate form of government, and anathematize every constitution founded on national sovereignty.]

I turn now to modern times. I look there for nations formed under our own eyes, or at least under perfect cognizance of their own consciousness. What example shall I take? Shall I go to Switzerland? Shall I question the commonwealth of the Lakes, the people of the glaciers, the sons of William Tell? Shall I tread again the dear paths of Belgium? No! let me cross the ocean, and stand in presence of that gigantic nation of which I have spoken. I am no courtier of the United States of America: thanks to my priestly office, I am no one's courtier. I am not even a blind admirer of them; and, if this were the proper place, I would warn them that they are slipping down the steep slope of moral decay, and that they will infallibly come, as we have come, to political and social decay. I would call them back to the better spirit of their early age, and to the genuine patriotism of their founders. This I may say, Gentlemen, I am a true son of Pius IX.; and Pius IX. has put honor on himself in sending his homage and his gift of a block of stone to the national monument to Washington. Oh, how grand that nation was! how grand it continues still! O people, thou art like the lion's whelp that is gone up to seize the prey! Thy prey is the wealth of both the hemispheres, thy proud independence, thy vast and fertile continent. Thou hast couched between the two oceans, in the shadow of thy lofty mountains, on the banks of thy rivers that are like seas! Thou hast roared like the lion; and like the lioness thou art slumbering in thy might. Who shall dare rouse thee up? *Quis suscitabit eum?**

Well, then, who is it that holds the sovereignty in this nation? None but itself. The very day when it

* Genesis, xlix. 9.

was born in pangs of travail, it grasped the sovereignty in its own bloody and jealous hands, and to this day it has not let it go. There every man is at once citizen and king.

[There is, then, such a thing as sovereignty—legitimate and to be respected—besides the sovereignty of absolute princes: the sovereignty of the nation itself, or democracy.

Can the nation which retains the sovereignty retain also the exercise of it? "Pure democracy," or power exercised directly by all the citizens, has been possible only in little republics like those of Greece, which were substantially nothing but sovereign villages; moreover, as has been excellently said, "the ancient commonwealth, gay but fragile flower, found the moisture of its root in slavery." In larger communities the people can exercise sovereignty only through representatives. This is *representative democracy*, whatever the form of it, republican or monarchical. Autocracy, that is, the right of commanding in its own name—in other words, absolute power—still resides in the hands of the nation; but the exercise of it is delegated to magistrates of its choice.

In presence of these two forms of sovereignty, which share between them the present of mankind, as they have shared the past, and doubtless are to share the future, Christianity has no choice to make, but one unvarying instruction to give. Be it man or nation that holds sovereign power on earth, this power is held only *in trust*. In truth, the sovereign is only the minister of God,* who alone is the real sovereign.]

PART SECOND.—*The Exercise of Sovereignty.*

Power is divine in its origin, and therefore inviolable. Power is human in its depositary, and therefore limited. These are the two laws of sovereignty, alike in the most absolute of monarchies and in the most radical of democracies.

I. Power is divine in its origin. "There is no power

* Romans, xiii. 1.

out of God." Every right, in fact, if it *is* a right, is derived from absolute reason and justice, which are only another name for God. A right purely human is simply absurd. When, therefore, I set up the claim to exact from my fellow-man a deference to my acts, however contrary they may be to his interests and preferences; when I undertake to put restraint upon his actions, and even on his person, by what I call my right, it is because I feel within me something that comes from above me, and which, for the time being, crowns me the sovereign of my fellow and my peer. Political power is a right in him who exercises it; it gives rise to duties in those who are subject to it. It is consequently divine just as all legitimate rights are divine, from the right of owner to that of husband or father; "for there is no power but of God."

Being divine, power is therefore inviolable and not to be resisted by any. Saint Paul himself comes to this conclusion: "Whosoever therefore resisteth the power, resisteth the ordinance of God;"* and he adds, "Wherefore ye must needs be subject, not only for wrath, but also for conscience' sake."† Ye are to bow yourselves, not to the might of the sword nor to the might of law, but to your own conscience. Might is not right, neither can man find within himself the ground of authority to command his fellow-man. But whenever your own conscience shows you your fellow-man in the majesty of right, then yield your obedience, not to man, but to God.

The principle of the inviolability of power belongs both to the doctrine and to the constant practice of the Catholic Church. We are permitted, many a time we are bound, to resist the abuses of power, but never to attack the power itself.

* Romans, xiii. 2.   † Ibid., xiii. 5.

It is the blunder and the crime of the French Revolution, that it erected into a principle what had theretofore been only a transient disorder in the life of nations—the overthrow of power. It has been said that it is time to make an end of the Revolution, and that, in order to end it, we must sit in judgment on it. Let me add, that in order to judge it, we must analyze it. If I take it at the start—at that famous date of 1789, I find before me two very different movements, which nevertheless are often confounded together. At the beginning, it was a legitimate and necessary reaction against the political abuses and moral corruption of the last days of the old *régime.* Political abuses had stifled, under an unprecedented centralization, the remains of the liberty of the Middle Ages, and the recent prosperity of the France of Henry IV. and Louis XIII. And as to moral corruption, my illustrious predecessor in this pulpit has depicted it with an admirable stroke of eloquence, courage, and truth: "In the room where Saint Louis had slept, Sardanapalus lay down! Stamboul was transported to Versailles, and there found itself entirely at home."* A shamefully large proportion of the provincial nobility, leaving behind them with their old-fashioned morals the scourge of absenteeism, hastened to follow or at least admire the new fashions in morality; and the court clergy united with them to sanction these corruptions, not, of course, in words—that would have been impossible—but by guilty silence. Against such a state of things, reaction could not be too energetic nor too indignant; but it should have continued to be peaceful and lawful. It was to reform the power, not destroy it. But what am I saying? The

---

* " *Conférences de Notre-Dame de Paris,* by the Reverend Father Lacordaire. XIIIe. Conf., De la Chasteté."

reform emanated from the power itself; and this generous initiative, sustained as it was by the vast majority of the country, made what I would call the 1789 of the honest king and the true French nation. Unhappily there was another 1789. The whole guilt does not rest on 1793; 1789 must bear its share of it. It is guilty of that contempt of authority, at once instinctive and systematic, which shows in its acts as well as in its ideas, which expressed itself sometimes in the wordy insurrection of the tribune, sometimes in the violent insurrection of the street, and which from the beginning opened the way for those who, having humbled the throne of the monarch before the National Assembly, finally erected his scaffold in front of his palace.

The French Revolution is now eighty years old, and it has come to be the European revolution. It has done enough in the way of destruction, it seems to me, and it is high time now to build up. Let us have done, then, with the shameful and perilous instability of our institutions, and to that end let us restore to its place in men's thoughts and consciences the Christian dogma of the inviolable sacredness of power.

[II. Sovereignty is limited in its exercise. If power is necessarily inviolable in its principle, which is divine, it is essentially limited in its exercise, which is human. All authority exercised by men has its limits, and those of civil authority are found in the *modality of rights* which it is its mission, as I have already explained, to regulate and defend. Political sovereignty no more extends to the substance of human rights when it is vested in the people than when it is vested in a prince; neither can it legitimately tamper with them, whether they be rights of the individual, rights of the family, the primitive society, rights of the Church, the superior society, or rights of voluntary associations. Every man has, by his own natural right, the power of associating himself with his fellows, so long as he does it openly and for objects not incompatible with morality and the public peace. Civil law has only one thing to do in this case: it has not to grant the right, but to acknowledge it.]

When civil authority oversteps these limits it is guilty of an abuse. It must be warned of it; if need be, it must be resisted. We are speaking, as it will be evident, not of insurrection, which is never "the holiest of duties," but of moral resistance, a resistance respectful toward the power, energetic against the abuses of power—the only permissible resistance, and the only effective.

The holy Scriptures present to us many fine examples of this legitimate protest of conscience against arbitrary and tyrannous government.

We read the gospel, and we do well; but we do not read the Old Testament as much as we ought—the history of that people Israel, of whom Moses says, in language full of mysterious significance, that it is the measure and type after which the other nations have been formed.*

For my own part, in studying these incomparable annals, from Judges to Maccabees, I have often been struck with a charming touch of nature, full of household poetry, full of social instruction: it is, that the peaceful tenure of the homestead is presented as the sign of the kingdom of God on earth. "Judah and Israel dwelt safely, every man under his vine and under his fig-tree."† The vine and the fig-tree; that is to say, the whole homestead, with all the outward belongings which constitute its comfort and its charm, and

---

* "When the Most High divided to the nations their inheritance, when he separated the sons of Adam, he set the bounds of the people according to the number of the children of Israel." Deuteronomy, xxxii. 8.

† 1 Kings, iv. 25.

that connection with nature which is so desirable, I was about to say so essential, to the idea of home.

Now in Israel, as in some other countries, public authority did not always respect the rights of private life. The book of Kings informs us that in the time of Ahab, a certain man had a vineyard in Jezreel, hard by the palace of the king. Ahab wanted this vineyard for a garden, and went himself to see Naboth, and said to him: "Give me thy vineyard and I will give thee for it a better vineyard; or, if it seemeth good to thee, I will give thee the worth of it in money."*

And Naboth said to Ahab, "The Lord forbid it me that I should give the inheritance of my fathers unto thee." To the mind of this simple man, full of the spirit of earlier days, it would have been an act of impiety to abandon the family home. The king of Israel paused and trembled before this assertion of the right of the family. "He came into his house," says the sacred text, "heavy and displeased; and he laid him down upon his bed, and turned away his face, and would eat no bread." Then his wife, Queen Jezebel, came in and asked the occasion of his trouble. And the king told her of his generous offer, and how it had been refused by that obscure working-man, and how that worthless bit of property had set itself in insurrection against the exigences of court splendor. "Truly," says Jezebel, with superb irony, "it's a marvellous authority that you hold, and grandly you govern the kingdom of Israel. Arise and eat bread, and I will give you the vineyard of Naboth the Jezreelite." So she wrote letters in Ahab's name, and sealed them with his seal, and commanded the elders of the city to execute swift and severe justice on a certain seditious per-

* 1 Kings, xxi. 1, 2.

son, Naboth, who had blasphemed God and the king. And on this occasion, as, alas, on so many others, the judges peeped under the sacred bandage of justice, and saw something more than justice itself. They cited Naboth before the people, and suborned two sons of Belial to bear witness against the innocent. The guiltless man was stoned. Jezebel, in triumph, said to Ahab, "Arise, take possession of the vineyard of Naboth the Jezreelite, which he refused to give thee for money: for Naboth is not alive, but dead." But while he was going toward that coveted estate, a man was waiting to meet him at the gate. Covered with the skins of wild beasts, with a leathern girdle about his loins, he had descended from the rocky heights of Carmel. A dweller in the desert, he respected the kingly majesty, but he braved the wrath of kings, when the kings trampled on the law of the Lord, and on the rights of their subjects. It was the prophet Elijah. Looking the usurper in the face, the prophet spake to the king: "Thou hast killed, and now thou hast taken possession. Robber and murderer, thus saith the Lord: In the place where dogs licked the blood of Naboth, shall dogs lick thy blood, even thine."*

This is liberty! It is the outcry of every honest man's conscience in face of the violation of a right. It is the protest of public opinion against the abuse of force, and the more perilous abuse of law.

[In conclusion, Father Hyacinthe remarked upon the error, now-a-days so common, of identifying the interests of liberty with questions of the form of government, which are necessarily secondary and subordinate to circumstances of time and place. It is not the *form* of power, but the *limits* of power, which it is

* 1 Kings, chapter xix.

important to define. In that direction lies, practically, the future of the world's liberty.]

The despotism of republics is as frequent, and more terrible than that of monarchies. Nothing equals the excesses of popular sovereignty when it begins to tamper with men's rights. The maxim of Lycurgus—for that matter, it was the common sentiment of all antiquity—was this: "that each citizen is the property of the country, and that as against the country he has no rights over himself." It is the identical doctrine which was enunciated in our day by the revolutionary Ruault, in the clean-cut and ferocious phrase, "All belongs to the State, body and goods."

To oppose itself to the encroachments of positive law, in the name of the unwritten law of human nature and of everlasting justice, has ever been the glorious mission of the Church, in Christian commonwealths. I am astounded, Gentlemen—I say it out of the fullness of my heart—I am astounded and grieved when I hear it said that the pope has preached sedition, because he has protested against the legal violation of the rights of the Church, which are also the natural rights of property. Such words as these affect to be liberal, but they are as much opposed to liberty as to reverence, and it is my duty to protest against them.

No, no! the Catholic Church, the Roman pontiff, do not commit an act of sedition when they say to the State, "You have no right to interfere with right." On the contrary, they perform an act of the most brave and loyal respect both to the State and to liberty. To speak and act thus is to glorify the State, for it is to maintain it in its noble frontiers, which are righteousness. It is to glorify us all; for it is to settle us upon our legitimate ground, which is liberty.

LECTURE THIRD.

December 15, 1867.

RELIGION IN THE LIFE OF NATIONS.

My Lord Archbishop and Gentlemen: We have recognized the divine right of power, whatever its particular form or its immediate origin; and in separating this doctrine from the exaggerated meaning ascribed to it by its adversaries and by a party of its defenders, we have affirmed, with the Apostle Paul, the supernal origin of all power, the inviolable and sacred character of all rights—rights of princes as well as citizens, rights of democracies as well as monarchies. "There is no power but of God."

But rights are not the only things which have within themselves an inspiration from on high. There is in political society something less definite but not less real: it is life; and to-day I am to inquire what part religion occupies in the life of nations.

None at all! is the answer of that sort of opinion, now-a-days so common, which would banish God from the social order, and which, though making up its mind to the speculative dogma of his existence, undertakes to crowd away his action into the recesses of the individual conscience, and to close against him all the gates of public life. They demand not only that the law should be atheist—which would certainly be quite too much to grant—but they ask the same for political ideas, for national morals, in a word, for the life of the country.

It is no part of my subject to examine in what degree civil legislation ought to connect itself with the existence of God in general or with Christianity in particular. At another time I shall come back to this important and complicated question, so much agitated of late. For the moment, then, I lay aside the subject of laws—a matter which belongs rather to the outward than to the interior structure of a nation. I waive the definite relations of Church and State, and taking things in their freer and profounder aspect, in religious creeds and public morals, I propose to prove that religion is the principle of national existence and prosperity.

I shall do this in two ways: first, by a general view, showing, not so much by reasoning as by history, how nations are constituted by their soul, and that this soul itself is quickened by religion; and then, with a more impressive particularity, tracing the action of the religious principle into the midst of the passions of public life, where it wakens and sustains those two forces the loss of which nothing else can make good—social justice and patriotic faith.

PART FIRST.—*Religion is the Superior Principle of National Life.*

[1. To begin with, Father Hyacinthe put the question, What is the true principle of national life?]

Is it the political organism, the positive laws of the established government? To see in the constitution of a nation this only or this chiefly, is to fall into the gross blunder of those who confound the life with the external organs of life. It is political materialism!

Is it, underneath these artificial limitations of laws and government, the more natural limitations of the soil—the course of the rivers, the conformation of the seas, the barriers of the mountains? These things may assuredly contribute to the perfect constitution of a nation, to its independence and its prosperity; and I am not one of those who fail to recognize the mysterious but purposed preparation of the globe with reference to the nations who were to dwell in it. But this element, also, is secondary. It enters into combination with others, or even disappears before them. How many great nations are there in Europe for which the natural frontiers have never been drawn!

Let us go a little deeper than these geographical or social forms. There is the blood, which gives character to the physical life; and the language, giving character to the moral life. Is it community of blood and language which constitutes a nation? Is it the race-principle? It is not for me to discuss the modern notion of nationalities. At this very hour it is condemned; condemned in theory by words full of authority, which have laid bare, from under the truths which it perverts, the error and peril which it covers; condemned in practice by the formidable events which have arisen, and before which the earth keeps silence!

What makes a nation is its soul. There is a soul in nations as in individuals, and this soul is their life.

A nation is a more or less considerable group of families, sprung sometimes of most diverse blood, but consciously united by one and the same public spirit. This people has a history in the past—not two histories, but one. Once let that living tradition be interrupted, and it is no longer the same people. It loses its identity. This people has a common conscience in the present, a common stock of beliefs, affections, interests, morals; and it is in the profound consciousness of this collective life that it declares its unity to itself, before declaring it to its rivals.

Now, in this national soul, I do not hesitate to say, the largest and best place belongs to religion. It is the essential law of the soul that it is constituted, in its nature and its proper life, by virtue of its relation with God. So that the materialists show their good sense when, in order to make an end of God, they seek, in the first place, to make away with the soul, both in the individual and in society. The soul of a people is, above all, its religion: it is this national worship of ours which (as some one so well expresses it) has held us in its embrace for twelve centuries, which has inspired our arts, our arms, our whole history, and which can be renounced only by renouncing with it the soul of the country.

[II. It is mainly by facts that we must convince an age which is all the time appealing from theory to facts. Father Hyacinthe seeks, therefore, in ancient and in contemporary history, the experimental proof of the alliance of the religious sentiment with the national sentiment. With this in view, he questions the history, successively, of the times before Christ, of the times after Christ, and finally of this present and doubtful hour of which the poet speaks—

"By what name shall we call thee, troubled hour
On which our fate is cast?"*

* "De quel nom te nommer, heure trouble où nous sommes?"
VICTOR HUGO.]

1. *History before Christ.*

The movement of humanity, like that of nature, is from East to West. It is from the East that the light comes, morning by morning. Thence we receive Christianity, the light of the soul. Thence, also, came the Aryan races, from which we are descended. Of what sort were these primeval communities? Theocracies, in which the national sentiment was so rooted in the religious sentiment, that the two were confounded together:—vast empires of Egyptians, Assyrians, Persians, whose first dynasties were composed of gods, whose lawgivers were priests, and who claimed to conquer their enemies less by force of arms than by the might of their divinities. Far beyond the regions in which these empires flourished, I perceive, in the remotest East, another, at once their contemporary and ours—China, that strange empire, the least religious in the world, and which, for that matter, comes nearest to the dreams of modern democracy. It is, in fact, an immense democracy, in which liberty is always willingly held subordinate to equality;—an authoritative democracy, disciplined under the mighty hand of a chief. It is the government, *ex officio*, of educated men. Instruction is not obligatory (and in this respect China is governed by a better inspiration than its imitators), but it penetrates none the less into the innermost recesses of the nation, and there it takes on those forms of "*independent morality*" which are so much preached up. It has pushed dogmas out of the way, southward toward India, northward toward Thibet. Scarcely has there been retained a vague, inoffensive deism; and the morality taught in the empire is, after that of Socrates, the noblest and purest of human moralities—that of Confucius. The most entire absence of prejudgments concerning the future life, united with a diligent and thrifty industry, makes China a model of social order, according to modern notions, possessing peacefully, by way of tradition, just what we are painfully reaching after by way of innovation. But now notice, for it is a marvellous fact, that in withdrawing private life from the influence of the religious idea, China has nevertheless deemed it impossible to establish the system of public life on anything but that idea. It claims to have relations with eternity; it calls itself the Celestial Empire, and its sovereign wears the title of the Son of Heaven.

[Returning from Asia to Europe, and pausing to consider the great civilization of the Romans, and its Sabine and Etruscan originals, Father Hyacinthe remarks their profoundly religious character.]

The manner in which cities were founded, according to the Etruscan rite, is an eloquent witness to the conviction then prevailing that the civil order has no other foundation than the religious order. The priests made a careful scrutiny of the site, and, marking off a mysterious spot in the centre of the enclosure, they dug there a pit in the form of the sky reversed. The lowest part of it was consecrated, *diis manibus,* to the gods of the departed, and the entrance of it was closed with a stone. This pit was called *mundus,* the world, and, according to the ideas of those nations, it was the communication between the visible and the invisible worlds, the outward affirmation of the fellowship of the living and the dead in one commonwealth. Thrice a year, the *mundus* was opened in solemn silence; public and private business was suspended, and the community beheld in its depths the secret of its origin and of its superhuman destiny.

Gods at its foundations—gods at its hill-tops—such was the old Italic commonwealth. It was from wells of tradition like these that Rome drew the *strength* that made her great, and became her enduring name. Founded by a gang of robbers and adventurers, she became the mistress of the world only when she had laid herself on her own altars, and consecrated the patriotism of her sons in acts of impassioned worship.

[Doubtless idolatry is a mad and guilty error. Nevertheless, under these perverted symbols were concealed great truths, often even great natural virtues, and this is the way in which it has been possible for false religions to contribute to the prosperity of families and States. Between the perversion of the religious sentiment, which is idolatry, and its utter extirpation, which is at the root of rationalism, patriotism cannot hesitate which to choose.]

2. *History since Christ.*

We are proud of our modern civilization, and with good reason; but we are not half enough familiar with the sources of it. A pen not less erudite than eloquent has lately exhibited them to us in a book which the future will think shame of us for having only half understood. I mean "The Monks of the West."* It is discovered that the history of these monks was the history of the West itself, and that in its cradle, if I might so speak, Europe was wrapped in monks' robes and grew up under their discipline. England, particularly, that classic land of liberty, has been plainly proved to be now bearing, in its institutions and its character, the lively impress of monastic life, the laws and usages of

---

* *Les Moines d'Occident,* by Montalembert.

those old cloisters by which it was founded, but which it has overthrown.

If it has been for a Catholic historian to remind England that she is the handiwork of her monks, it has been for an English Protestant historian to show France, in the course of the last century, that she is the handiwork of her bishops. On a field of battle, in the heart of a hero, the patriotism of Franks became wedded to the faith of Christians. Their alliance was sealed by the hand of Saint Remigius, and from the soul of Clovis it passed to the soul of the whole nation. From that time forth this alliance has run the gauntlet of the centuries, defying prosperity to corrupt, and misfortune to subdue it. . . . Let me call to mind Joan of Arc—a name that can never grow commonplace to the ears of Frenchmen. "When Paris falls, all history shows that France is fallen." When Chateaubriand wrote these words, he did not remember Joan of Arc. The king of England was reigning here almost uncontested, and Charles VII., settled down into the "king of Bourges," was gayly celebrating the funeral of the French monarchy by the inauguration of the era of royal mistresses. Who shall be the savior of France? A country-girl, simple and pure as nature and the people in whose bosom she had been reared, and, like them, religious. She listened to the murmur of the bells; she gazed into the sky. Beneath the beech-tree of Domremi she heard voices speaking to her of God and France, and commissioning her, not to bring back the king to Paris, but to cause him to be anointed at Rheims.

[In order to completeness, it would be needful to run over the entire history of the Christian nations in their best epochs. This would demonstrate at every turn the alliance, or rather the fusion of the religious and the national sentiments. Father Hyacinthe referred to Spain, now fallen, once so great; the heroic and sometimes age-long struggles of its religious patriotism against the Moors; and that national epopee which closed amid the splendors of Isabella and Ferdinand the Catholic—an epoch in which Spain was the first nation of Europe.]

3. *Contemporary Nations.*

Contemporary nations are no exception to this established law. Notwithstanding the crisis that some of them are passing through, Christianity continues among them to be the controlling influence over public character, and the inspirer of national feeling. Nothing can be more contrary to a just and careful observation of Europe and America than the opinion, so common amongst us, that the religious element has been eliminated from national life.]

We hear a great deal said about Germany, and sometimes there are those who remark with dismay upon her formidable growth at our very gates. Well, Gentlemen, France has nothing to fear from Germany in the matter of material power. Neither has it anything to borrow from Germany in the way of that pantheist or materialist philosophy against which Germany itself has reacted. What I admire among the Germans is their reverence for home, their respected and cherished traditions of family life, and, despite the stubborn efforts of skepticism and revolution, their national faith in Jesus Christ and his gospel.

* * * * *

The school of opinion against which I am contending thinks that it finds in the United States an example and model of the separation of the religious and the national life. I do not know a more complete mistake. What is separated in the United States is the State and the Church, or rather the churches which that country reckons up without number: and in that state of things it could not be otherwise. But if religion has nothing to do there with legislation, it has much to do with public character. The scourge of rationalism which desolates all Europe is known there only in rare and exceptional cases; public opinion rejects it as not less contrary to the prosperity of the nation than to the welfare of the soul. The courts of justice refuse with horror the testimony of an avowed atheist.* . . . Thus the most perspicacious of those French publicists who make democracy to consist in the exclusion from civil society of all religious influence, refuse to acknowledge the American Union as "a perfect democracy," and make against it this bitter reproach: "that the American commonwealth is not satisfied with philosophy, but that it admits one as a citizen only on condition of his being a Christian."†

[Father Hyacinthe concluded the historical argument by the example of two nations whose rare privilege it has been to unite the sympathies both of Catholic and of Liberal opinion—Poland and Ireland. Politically, these two nations are dead; they live only in their soul, and their soul is wholly wrapt up in Catholicism. This is declared in eloquent terms by their orators and poets, and more loudly yet, by the very nature of the odious oppression they have suffered.]

PART SECOND.—*Religion the Principle of Social Justice and Patriotic Faith.*

[Father Hyacinthe proposed, next, to give the reason for what he had proved to be the universal fact.]

Why is it that the soul of a people subsists mainly on God and religion? Strictly speaking, it is enough to

---

* *New York Spectator*, August 23, 1831; quoted by de Tocqueville.
† *La Démocratie*, by M. Vacherot, pp. 34, 35.

have proved the fact. The fact is conclusive of itself, as soon as it is established. But I wish to penetrate with you to the roots of this fact. I wish to define the principal functions of religion in the domain of public life. These functions are chiefly to maintain social justice and create patriotic faith.

I. Social Justice. We have seen, Gentlemen, that in the political system two great forces come together—Power and the People. These are two great forces, and at the same time, two great rights. We have refuted the narrow conception of certain publicists who recognize in the right of power, a right exceptionally divine. The right of power is "of God," but just as all other rights are from him. There are, then, rights divine, and consequently sacred and inviolable, in that multitude of individuals that make up a people—in that group of families and homes which we call a nation. There are rights in the individuals, in the families, in the nation itself; and besides these, there are rights in the power. And because all these rights are vested in human hands—blind, passionate—they are liable to be brought together in terrible collisions.

Ah, how needful, in the midst of society, that there should be some moral power to rise up and prevent or appease these collisions! Political society needs it even more than domestic society. Harmony exists by natural law in the family; antagonism exists by natural law in the State. Harmony exists by natural law between husband and wife, between father and child. Order in the family springs from the loins of fatherhood; it germinates with love in the bosom of mother and child; it grows out of the coalition of all the interests and affections of human nature. But in the State, this is no longer true. On the one side are the temptations of power—the most formidable that I know of in the world. A man, or men—no matter which—an individual person or a collective person, but any way a person possessing unlimited power, since it rests with one hand on law, and with the other on force—since it has only to will, and there are set in motion millions of beings, and the world receives an impulse and direction which controls, more or less, the future itself; how, in such a case, can there help forming little by little, and rising to the heart, that intoxication of pride, and of the foremost pride of all, the pride of power? Pleasure has been called the great passion of human nature. It is a mistake. The great passion is domination. To this, men sacrifice everything, even pleasure, when pleasure stands in the way of it.

And in face of these encroachments of power, in face of that towering pride in the hearts of sovereigns ("their pride ascending forever"),* there is another sort of pride not less detestable, other sorts of outrage not less terrible. A people weary with always obeying, with toiling much, and suffering much: a people which looks upward, and first envies and then threatens! Chained, like Samson to his grinding in the prison-house, like him it perceives the growing locks of strength upon its brow, it heeds its swelling veins, and the vital sap of manhood in its heart. Now its turn has come; it grows drunken with the wine of its wrath, and reckless of its own ruin, it pulls down the pillars of the edifice which is to crush itself and its oppressors together.

O men and brethren, gaze upon this great ocean of human society! Behold these two great waves that heave themselves from its depths—the wave of the People and the wave of the Sovereign. They mount,

* Psalm lxxiv. 23. (Vulgate version.)

they swell, they crest themselves and roar! If nothing check them, they shall dash themselves against each other with a thunder-crash! And now before these two waves, these two conflicting oceans in the same bed, lay down that grain of sand of which Jehovah speaks: "Thus far shalt thou come, and no farther." Ocean of Power, Ocean of Multitude, abase your wrath, humble all your pride before this powerless but divine boundary of duty!

Religion is the only thing which can put self-devotion into the heart of governments and respect into the hearts of the people. It is hard for government long to deny itself; it is hard for the people always to yield respect. But the Lord Jesus has said to human governments—Of old, the kings of the nations have been called from among the mighty, and have wielded lordly dominion over them. Henceforth it shall not be so. Henceforth kings shall be but ministers, and "he that would be greatest must make himself servant of all."*

Christ alone could make such promises. Christianity alone, by inspiring governments with practical and lasting devotion, could fulfil them. Christianity alone has been able to hold the people steadily to their allegiance. It alone has been able to speak thus to them and get a hearing: "There is nothing that you cannot do, but nothing that it is right for you to do. Ye are to be subject, not for wrath's sake, but for conscience' sake, not only to the just and upright prince, but also to the froward."

I am right, then, in saying, with our holy Book, that righteousness is the salvation of nations, and that Christianity has for its mission upon earth to establish the kingdom of social as well as individual righteousness.

* Matthew, xx. 27.

Machiavelli is wrong, and his disciples with him. No Government can long stand supported on one side by force, on the other by cunning. The time will come when it will encounter one stronger and shrewder than itself, and will find, too late, that what preserveth and "exalteth a nation" is righteousness.

And this is why the Catholic Church has always proclaimed that the laws of morality were laws not only for private but for public life; that the Ten Commandments of Moses and the Gospel of Jesus Christ were made not only for individuals but for nations; and that citizens and monarchs, social rights and social powers, hold alike of justice and of God.

And this is why I, standing here, am right, whatever timorous and complaining souls may think, in teaching these truths of which the world has need.

I am right in taking in my hands "the everlasting Gospel," unfolding it in all its breadth, and crying aloud, like the apocalyptic angel, to kings and peoples, without respect of person, to all the dwellers upon earth, Righteousness! Righteousness! and again Righteousness!

[II. Patriotic Faith. To love and serve one's country, it is needful to have faith in it, and this is inspired by religion.]

The heart of man is so made that it loves ardently and long only when it feels a breath of divine inspiration in its love. This inspiration may be abused, but there can be no true love without it. If I saw in my country nothing but an institution of human contrivance, a sort of social clock-work whose numberless little wheels are ticketed off in the Bulletin of Laws and set in motion by the myriad hands of the bureaucracy; if I saw in it nothing but a patch of common earth occupied by people foreign, and sometimes hostile to each other, how could such a France as that waken in my heart one throb of enthusiasm? The false prophet of Italian revolution reproaches his country with being materialist. He would have it religious; or rather, he would have it *a religion.** And so do I, but in a better sense, desire France to be a religion.

I desire it for two reasons: because this religion of patriotism will give us strength to sacrifice to it personal selfishness; and because it will give us wisdom to subordinate to it humanitarian sentiment.

1. *Personal Selfishness.*

An illustrious patriot has said, "Remember that love of country is sacrifice, not enjoyment." When love is enjoyment, it is very easy; but it is often, then, nothing but selfishness. But when love costs one the persevering sacrifice of everything, O what need for it to rest on faith—faith profound, enthusiastic!

Such is love of country. We have to obey laws which trammel us; we have to give up, not our rights, indeed, but the personal, independent way of exercising our rights. Positive law says to us, "I shall not interfere with your right; but, that you may not encroach on your neighbor's right, you must exercise your own under such and such limitations and conditions." Then, after the yoke of the law, there comes down on us the burden of taxation, falling alike on the penury of the poor and the superfluity of the rich. And then, after the taxation of property, the draft upon person and blood— a necessary thing, but a cruel;—cruel to the father, from whom it snatches the companion of his labors;

---

* The Religious Side of the Italian Question, by Joseph Mazzini. *Atlantic Monthly*, October, 1867.

to the mother, from whom it tears the joy of the little home; and to the young man himself, from whom it takes away the noblest period of his free and blooming youth.

All these sacrifices the faith of patriotism—that is, the national sentiment purified and transfigured by religion—counts as nothing. It leads the soldier to the field of carnage, there to fight like a hero, and to die like a Christian. Let me cite one instance of it, to the honor of our enemies; those were enemies grand even in defeat, and their valor magnified our victory. Well, on the field of Inkermann, the battle over, when they came to observe the dead with that regard for science which is not inconsistent with a tender heart, the surgeons were struck with the look of religious and almost ecstatic serenity impressed upon the faces of the Russian dead.

2. *The Humanitarian Sentiment.*

[Father Hyacinthe remarked that, in our days, patriotic faith has not, as formerly, to react only against personal selfishness, but against the perversion of that sentiment, otherwise so just and noble, the humanitarian sentiment.]

When I was yet a boy, I used to read those noble lines of one of our greatest poets:

> " Ye nations! (pompous name for savage hate!)
> Can love be halted at your boundary-lines?
> Tear down those envious flags! and hear the voice—
> That other voice—that speaks this stern reproach:
> 'Self-love and hate alone possess a country,
> But brotherly love has none.' "*

> * Nations! mot pompeux pour dire barbarie!
> L'amour s'arrête-t-il où s'arrêtent vos pas?
> Déchirez ces drapeaux; une autre voix vous crie:
> L'égoïsme et la haine ont seuls une patrie,
>   La fraternité n'en a pas!
>   DE LAMARTINE, *La Marseillaise de la paix.*

These are fine lines; but they are false, and their generous but fatal illusion has too much affected the minds of our fellow-citizens. They may not "tear down" their flag, but they lower it. They unlearn true patriotism, not by loving humanity too well, but by loving it unwisely.

If I were to indulge myself in the *argumentum ad hominem*, I should have an easy time of it. I should say to the philosophic and revolutionary school: You have been accusing us, till within a few years—us Christians, and especially us Catholics—of not comprehending the love of country; of extirpating it, or at least drying it up in the heart! You have been telling us that we could not love an earthly country, because we did nothing but dream of a heavenly one:—that we could not serve our native land, because we were laboring for the universal Church. You have been telling us these things, flinging against us these unjust reproaches, to which our whole history makes answer; and now, forsooth, you yourselves are setting humanity in the place of the Church, and under our very eyes are sacrificing to it the interests of your country, and (though you may not suspect it) its honor also.

[In conclusion, Father Hyacinthe referred to the example of the typical people. Nothing could be more religious than the national sentiment of Israel, and therefore, by a beautiful necessity, nothing more genuinely humanitarian.]

I have spoken of all the rest of the nations, but said nothing of Israel. Nevertheless, this people has possessed, in the highest degree, the two spirits which make up a nation;—the spirit of the hearth, and the spirit of the altar—the two sanctuaries which religion occupies or deserts at the same time. Israel was a family, and its people was called "the house of Jacob." It preserved in its public archives the genealogy of its fathers, and, as I might say, a complete history of its blood. It knew how, from the heart of its first ancestor, by the veins of the twelve patriarchs as by so many sacred channels, the blood which God had blessed had flowed downward to itself. The twelve tribes remained distinct, almost independent, and yet united; and in each of them each family maintained the sovereignty of its own home. Every fifty years, at the solemn jubilee, the homestead, that might have been sold under some pinch of necessity, reverted to its former owners. The old home seemed to leap for joy as it welcomed them back; and on the spot where the grandsire had been wont to dwell, he joyfully greeted his descendants.

And to the domestic spirit, what people has better united the religious spirit? It was God's own people. Its city was a temple, the holy hill of Zion. Its history, its poetry, its laws were all contained in the inspired book. Its sages spoke to it in the name of the Lord; in his name its kings held empire and its warriors fought its holy wars.

Now, this obscure people, that had to choose between the oblivion of the world and its contempt, this petty State, whose breadth was not more than twenty leagues, is that one of all the world which has rendered the greatest service to mankind. To it humanity owes everything, from that idea—not Shemitic, but Hebrew—which gives its nobleness and strength to modern thought, the idea of the one, personal, and living God, down to that mysterious blood of Calvary, which alone has power to fecundate the divine idea that out of it should come forth the virtues which have converted and civilized our fathers, and founded Christian society.

4

In vain Socrates had taught and died. Athens and Rome still kept their ancient gods and their ancient character. If we, this day, are living in a Christian land, it is because the sons of Judah have come bringing to us the treasure preserved through so many centuries in the close, jealous, but beneficent casket of their national independence.

LECTURE FOURTH.

December 22, 1867.

THE HIGHER INTERCOURSE BETWEEN NATIONS.

GENTLEMEN: I am about to touch upon one of the grandest ideas of the higher politics. And I have a perfect right to do it, if it were only by way of retaliation; for the idea itself touches upon the gravest questions of morality and religion.

I have been speaking thus far of the nation; but there are *the nations*. I am about to inquire whether there are not bonds existing between them which unite them into one universal society.

What was it that made men feel the need of some bond superior to domestic society? It was the multitude of families. If human nature had been able to limit itself to that grand primeval unity which constituted it one single family under the sceptre of Adam, there would have been no occasion for civil society. Now, the nations are many, as the families were; consequently, it would seem that they have need, for the same reason, to have set up over them an arbitration accepted by all, and so recover harmony without losing liberty, in the bonds of a broader fellowship.

Is there, then, any higher fellowship among nations;

and what is the nature of the bond that constitutes it? Is it a political bond? Is it simply a moral bond? Is it a religious bond? These are the three aspects under which this important subject is to be considered.

I can hardly keep myself from a certain emotion as I approach it. It brings back to me those enthusiasms of my early youth which I shared in common with my fellows. The commonwealth of mankind appeared to me then in the shadows of immature and undefined speculation; I had a poor enough conception of what it is in itself, and what it may grow to be under the action of Christianity; and yet I felt my heart of hearts answering to that conception with inexpressible yearnings. At this day, thank God, I see it in that perfect light which is poured upon earthly as well as upon heavenly things by the Catholic synthesis. I believe I love it better; I want to serve it better; and in this light which does not mislead, I will attempt, Gentlemen, to consider it with you.

PART FIRST.—*The Political Bond.*

And, first, is there any political bond adapted to form among all the States of the globe a cosmopolitan commonwealth? If no such bond exists at present, may it peradventure exist in the future?

Why not? What is the State itself if not a political bond between States less than itself?

Civil society is not so simple as it would seem to be at first sight. It is composed of three concentric spheres —three planes, one above another; at the base, the township; above that the province; at the top, the State.

1. The township is the starting-point of that wonderful organization which, together, makes up civil society. If I except that ideal and miraculous people, that Israel which has anticipated the progress of the centuries, I find civil society nowhere in all the East. I find there lordships, principalities, potentates, swaying over the multitudes a sceptre under which are mingled, in disproportionate and fantastic fashion, the authority of the father over his family and the authority of the master over his slaves. But the community, the free association of families, that glorious germ of genuine civilization, we do not find till we set foot on the soil of the West, its native soil, and pause before the creative race of the children of Japheth. Such are the democratic cities of Greece; such, especially, is the *civitas* of the Romans.

I am no panegyrist of the Roman law. On the contrary, I think that its excessive influence has been one of the misfortunes of the Latin nations, and I prefer to it, for more than one reason, the "common law" of the Germanic race. But no one can refuse to this legislation the glory of having been the first to formulate the principles of civil society; and for my part, I subscribe with all my heart to the eulogy pronounced on it by the Apostolic Constitutions, that venerable monument of the primitive Church: "God has not chosen that his justice should be manifested to us alone, but that it should be resplendently displayed, also, in the Roman laws." For, as Saint Augustine adds: "In like manner as God has spoken supernaturally by the prophets, he has also spoken naturally by the Roman lawgivers. *Leges Romanorum divinitus per ora principum emanarunt.*"

Civil society was so identified with Rome, that when

the deluge of barbarians had swept over the empire, nothing remained of it but ruins. After that there began to reappear, with better races and under novel forms, mitigated withal by Christianity, that reign of chieftaincies of which Asia is the cradle. Those in whom the government was vested were called *lords*. It was the reign of the castle, the preponderance of the domestic element over the civil. . . . In what way did life come back into civil society? Under the floating wrecks, the waves, the drifting sea-weeds of that ocean of barbarians, the germ of the Roman municipality had survived. When the hour of Providence had struck, this germ flourished anew. It fructified in France, in Italy, everywhere, under the dawning sun of the Middle Age, under the vernal breath of modern civilization. But there is no need that I should recount here the glorious history of *the towns*.

[2. Such is the first sphere of civil society. But the towns are many, and have need to be united without losing their proper existence. Hence the necessity of *the province*.]

The too little remembered history of our past bears witness, and the actual practice of the free and prosperous nations of Europe confirms the testimony of history, that between those two centres of national activity, the restricted centre of the town and the immense centre of the State, there is always wanted an intermediate centre. Call it by what name you like. I am satisfied with the name transmitted to us by history—*Provincia*, the province. Originally, no doubt, a name of the vanquished, whether of the empire or of the feudal power; but afterward a triumphal name, the first and liveliest expression of a spirit of race, and an historical tradition in the formation of new nations.

I know that, thus speaking, I run against the prejudices of that revolutionary school which calls itself *liberal*, but is anything else but that. I do not defy it, but I am not afraid of it; and in the name of truth, of the interests of France, and the traditions of Europe, in the name of the future as well as of the past, I repeat, *we must have provinces*. We must have intermediate centres, to react on the one hand against the division and anarchy of the towns, and on the other against the centralization of the State. Let us then no longer neglect the conditions of provincial life. Alongside of the national language, let us have the originality of their antique idiom, which we call so scornfully a *patois*, the richness and simplicity of their ancient costumes, their simple and religious character, the guardian of all domestic and patriotic virtues. Let us remember that if the Church, without impairing the unity of which she is so justly jealous, has been able, in all lands and in every time, to tolerate and even encourage within her pale the most amazing variety,* then national unity has no more occasion to dread the free development of provincial life.

[3. The State, the central and sovereign power, unites then the provinces without confounding them, and so forms the third bond of civil society.]

I admire the State, when it abides within its natural limits. I praise it; I am so content with it that I do not care to look for anything further. Town needed to be united to town. It was needful that, without losing their independence and autonomy, the united towns should become the province. And in turn, the

---

* *Circumdata varietate .... circumamicta varietatibus.* (Psalm xlv. 9, 14.) Acts of Pius IX. relating to the Oriental Liturgies.

province, looking about on its sister provinces, needed to join hands with them and form that august circle which we call by the name of France. But higher in the scale than France, I find, in the political order—nothing—nothing!

In fact, what could I find? If I looked into the past, I should find universal empire. If I looked into the future—no, not the future—if I looked into Utopia, I should find national confederation. No, no, Gentlemen, neither one nor the other of these; neither universal empire nor confederation of nations, but France.

Universal empire I need not speak of. I hate to think of it. I would rather leave it to itself, in the bare facts of history, from Nebuchadnezzar down to Cæsar and his modern imitators. Gory spectre that it is, it seems to say, like Macbeth in Shakspeare's tragedy,

> "What hands are here! Ha! they pluck out mine eyes!
> Will all great Neptune's ocean wash this blood
> Clean from my hand?"

If universal empire is such a dismal nightmare, national confederation is a harmless and laughable chimera, not worthy the honor of a refutation. There exists, it is true, a confederation of the United States of America. There has been talk, sometimes, in noble but utopian phrase, of the confederation of the United States of Europe; but no one dreams of the confederation of the United States of the globe. I pause here, therefore, and conclude this first discussion with the declaration that there neither has been in the past, nor is to be in the future, any political body superior to the nation.

And if, after having looked manward for the evidence of this fact, I look Godward for the ultimate reason of it, I acknowledge that he has dealt with the nations of the earth with a higher respect than they have sometimes used toward themselves. He has wished them to be free and sovereign; he has given them into no mortal hands, but only to his Son, when he said to him, "Ask of me, and I will give thee the nations for thine inheritance, the uttermost parts of the earth for thy possession."*

The Word made flesh has asked of the Father. The Word of righteousness and truth has received the kingdom. The question is settled. The nations, liberated by this Word, belong only to themselves, and God.

PART SECOND.—*The Moral Bond.*

[Having proved that the nations are not, among themselves, in a state of political society, Father Hyacinthe proposes to show that they are united in *natural* society by moral bonds. The idea of the "social compact" is as false for nations as for individuals; and it is of sovereign importance, in the present question, not to confound the "state of nature" with the savage state.]

Before the foundation of civil society, individuals were not in "the state of nature," but in the state of domestic society. It was the *families* which, for lack of some higher bond, dwelt together in the state of nature. And yet their relations were not left to the control of violence and cunning—to the reign of barbarism. On the contrary, this was the noble period of the patriarchs. The various families, free from the trammels of social life and from the passions which it engenders, pure and happy in their manners, grand and simple in their way of living, realized the golden age of domestic society. Nations, with respect to each other, are in a situation analogous to that of families not yet

* Psalm ii. 8.

subject to civil society. Their relations are subject to the higher law of morality and the unwritten constitution of the law of nations. Consequently, they form among themselves a real though invisible commonwealth, which I will call the universal commonwealth of international justice.

I have been telling you, lately, that there is such a thing as justice for public life as well as for private life—for society as well as for the individual. To-day I complete the glorious survey; I reach the highest point, and declare that above that social justice which regulates the relations between government and people, there is an international justice presiding over the relations between nation and nation.

God (as I was but just now saying) has treated the nations with great honor, in that he has left them free: he has treated them with higher honor still, in that he has subjected them to law. It was not exclusively for the individual conscience, it was not only for the people of Israel, that God dictated the Ten Commandments to Moses; it was for all mankind. O man, look upon thy Lawgiver. Not now toward Israel, but toward thee, he descends from the smoking top of Horeb, the two rays upon his brow, the two tables in his hand. It is to every kindred and tongue that he proclaims the everlasting law. It is to nations and sovereigns that he says, "Ye shall not kill." Ye shall not make men's lives the tools of your revenge and your ambition. Ye shall not pour out their blood like water on the barren furrows of your battle-fields. Ye shall make no unjust wars; and if war comes persistently knocking at the door of your cabinets, ye shall ponder it long and scrupulously in the scales of conscience. Ye shall not kill.

Further; ye shall not steal. Ye shall steal neither kingdoms nor provinces. What is forbidden to a private individual is still more forbidden to a nation or a sovereign. What would you think of a private individual who, finding his vineyard or his field too strait for his wants or for his comfort and convenience, should seriously demand of his neighbor a rectification of frontiers? What would you say of a private person who, looking forth from the midst of his vast estate upon some intruding angle of another's property, of ancient date and venerable association, should say to the proprietor, " Your castle is the natural capital of my domain. If you don't give it to me, I'll take it, or I'll have it taken?" " Ye shall not steal," says the Law to governments as well as individuals, to nations as well as monarchs.

It adds, moreover, " Ye shall not bear false witness against your neighbor." Ye shall not lie through the penetrating voice of the press, after ye have lied in the secret whispers of diplomacy. Ye shall not pervert the conscience of the people. Ye shall not make use of calumny, in default of force, against the rights of the small and weak.

This is international justice. This is the sacred bond which constitutes and sustains the commonwealth of nations.

Some day history will be written, I am sure, as it is not written now, as it never has been written yet—for under other forms the evils which afflict us have afflicted our fathers before us—history will learn, at last, to speak the truth. It will say that such iniquities are not to be condoned by success; that not success, but justice is the law of nations; finally, that such acts as these are not glory, but national robbery.

History, too, will define better than it has been wont to do the boundaries between civilization and barbarism. I made a mistake, some time ago, speaking on this subject before another audience in Belgium. I attempted to define these limits, looking for them too exclusively from the religious point of view. Said I, "The Rubicon which one cannot cross without falling into barbarism is baptism. The baptized nations (whether Catholic or not, they are at least Christian) are the kernel of civilization; the unbaptized nations are the vast zone of barbarism." ... But history will say that the reign of civilization prevails throughout the whole domain of earth which acknowledges the authority of that axiom of international justice, Right makes Might. And as for barbarism, its empire begins with the empire of that other maxim, Might makes Right.

PART THIRD.—*The Religious Bond.*

[I. International law establishes between nations a society which is real, but without positive organization. Father Hyacinthe affirms that the outward and visible bond which is wanting to this society may be supplied by the universal religious society—in other words, by the Catholic Church.]

One does not easily lay off the sentiments of early life. As for myself, I acknowledge myself faithful to the dream of my boyhood. Even now I want to see with my eyes and touch with my heart the unity of my race, organized and living on the earth. I fight against the illusions of the humanitarians, but I love and serve the great truth which they pervert.

[Father Hyacinthe observed that just as domestic societies are united, not by a bond of the same order with themselves, but by the bond of the political order, so the various political societies must seek their unity, not in a bond of like nature, but in the higher bond of the religious order. Universal religious society alone can realize the organic unity of the nations, without infringing or even threatening their legitimate autonomy.]

This universal society of souls and of nations is the Catholic church. In evidence of this, I call to witness its name, as illustrated by facts. Whereinsoever other religious communions are worthy of respect, I honor them. Far from putting odium upon them, I have given them my hand—I give it still. But they are themselves the first to acknowledge—sometimes even to claim it as a merit—that they have no pretension to universality. Less absolute than we, they deem it a duty to make terms with circumstances of time and place, with the genius of races and the exigences of governments. Some of them — the unestablished churches—appeal to individuals, or at most to families. The others—State churches—seek to identify themselves with nations. None of them has the boldness to proclaim itself the Church of Humanity, or to say, like us, "Out of my pale, wilfully abandoned by one who knows what he is doing and means it—out of my pale there is no salvation."

Ah! I have found at last the bond of national unity, the tie of the perfect organization of mankind upon the earth! I grasp it in my trembling hands. This bond is not political, and consequently, sooner or later, tyrannical. It is a spiritual and unarmed bond, the strength of which proceeds from God and has its seat in the soul. The nations have nothing to fear from it, and everything to hope.

When the immortal King of the Catholic church appeared before Pilate, who represented the political power of that time, the Roman governor anxiously inquired concerning his title to royalty. "Art thou a King, then?" he asked. And Jesus answered, "Thou sayest it; I am a King." But he added, "My kingdom is not of this world." His kingdom, indeed, is in this world, or rather it enters into it, but it comes to it from above, and returns thither whence it came. It leaves to Cæsar that which is Cæsar's—that is to say, the politics of this world. It claims for God that which is God's—that is, the conservation of righteousness.

[II. Having shown that the Catholic Church alone, by virtue of being a society at once universal and spiritual, is capable of realizing the unity of nations, Father Hyacinthe inquired how this work was accomplished by it. He answered, chiefly in two ways: 1, by becoming the higher and divine organ of national as well as individual morality; 2, by creating, through the influence of religion, common interests and sentiments in the different peoples, and, so to speak, a universal country, which unites all countries in itself without confounding them. It is thus that it has realized that wonderful expression of Saint Paul, "that the nations should be fellow-heirs, and of the same body, and partakers of his promise in Christ by the gospel."* The nations are more than copartners; they are "*concorporeal*"—forming but one body in Jesus Christ.

The limits of this report do not permit us to enter into the development which Father Hyacinthe gave of these two positions. We shall simply present the conclusion of this discussion, and of the discourse itself.]

Cosmopolitan society has two centres—each of them a religious centre—Jerusalem and Rome: Jerusalem, which has prepared everything; Rome, which is to complete everything. These are those mysterious cities of which the prophet says, in his profound and forcible language, that they are like "the navel of the earth."† Separating from them, humanity forgets its own begin-

---

* Ephesians, ii. 6.   † Ezekiel, xxxviii. 12. See marginal translation.

nings, and makes schism with its principle of life and unity. The miracle of the union of nations, like that of the union of souls, has been possible only in the alliance of Jerusalem and Rome.

The call of the Gospel and the Church is addressed not only to souls, but to nations; as the very language of the Scriptures implies—"the conversion of the nations."* Perhaps Christian thinkers have not sufficiently pondered the fact of the blessing of all the *nations* of the earth, promised to the seed of Abraham, and fulfilled in the blood of Jesus."†

However this may be, at the hour when this promise was about to be accomplished—when the nations were more than ever hungering and thirsting, not for the Roman unity which was crushing them, but for that better unity which they dimly discovered, not knowing by what name to call it—there was at Cesarea a centurion of the Italian school, named Cornelius, a devout man, born in the darkness of paganism, but seeking God in all the uprightness of his heart and mind. While he was praying, an angel of the Lord drew near to him and said, "Cornelius, thy prayers and alms are come up for a memorial before God. And now send men to Joppa, and call for one Simon Peter, who is lodging at the sea-side, at the house of one Simon, a tanner. He shall tell thee what thou oughtest to do." And the centurion chose three trusty men, and dispatched them to this first pope of the universal Church, whose utterance the angel from heaven had not ventured to anticipate.

Simon Peter was hungry; and while they were making ready his repast, he was praying on the house-top. when

---

* Acts, xv. 3. "Gentiles" — "nations."
† Genesis, xxii. 18; xxvi. 4. Acts, iii. 25.

he fell into a trance. He saw heaven opened, and as it had been a great sheet knit at the four corners let down to earth, wherein (strange sight!) were those unclean animals which the law of Moses had forbidden to be eaten—four-footed beasts, and creeping things, and fowls of the air. And there came a voice to him, "Rise, Peter; kill and eat." "Not so, Lord," cried the zealous Jew, "for I have never eaten anything that is common or unclean." And the voice spake unto him again the second time, "What God hath cleansed, that call not thou common." And three times this mysterious vessel was let down and received up again into heaven. And when Peter had come forth from his trance, the three men were standing before the gate; and the Holy Spirit spoke to his inward soul, "Follow them, nothing doubting, for I have sent them."*

Gentlemen, this vision has been continued from age to age. It is the whole history of the Church and the papacy. Like the first of their number, the Roman pontiffs have beheld the nations, not now in the vessel let down from heaven, but on the agitated soil of this world. Here, the corrupted beasts of imperial Rome; there, the ferocious beasts of Scythia and Germany: the former panting after pleasure, and filling the air with their most beastly cry, "*Panem atque circenses*"—despotism, if you like, but give us our food and our amusements! the latter panting after carnage, craving blood, and preparing vengeance for the detested empire.

The first look, perhaps, was one of horror; the second, one of love. The papacy rose up before these monsters and slew them one by one. With the sword of the word, it struck at the unclean principle, in their bosom, of the life of sin, selfishness, pride, and sensuality. And

* Acts, x. 1–33.

then it devoured them. Slowly but steadily, century after century, it has been laboriously incorporating them into Christ, into that great Christendom of Charlemagne and Gregory VII., from which we are descended. And despite the blasphemies of our blind and unthankful age, it will prolong this splendid banquet of Christianity and civilization. "Rise, Peter, kill and eat." Yea, rise, O thou who art not only pontiff of the individual conscience, and of the family hearth, but pontiff of all the nations! Bishop of bishops, rise with all thy brethren! Rise, O Catholic hierarchy! Rise, Church of mankind, kill and eat! Incorporate in God, in truth and in righteousness, the nations once rebellious, now gratefully submissive!

And there shall come a day—never has it seemed more remote than now to shallow minds, never to believing hearts has it appeared so near—a day when, the mighty work achieved, the pontiff shall look forth upon mankind, not with more of love, but with more of joy than ever before, and say, My son! And as with one voice and one heart, mankind shall say, My father!

In that day the infallible promises of God shall have met, in their accomplishment, the ceaseless aspirations of man. Then unity shall be complete. There shall be one fold and one shepherd. For this I look, and am certain.

LECTURE FIFTH.

DECEMBER 29, 1867.

WAR.

My Lord Archbishop, and Gentlemen: If I glance backward at the way over which we have come, I mark our starting-point on the line between domestic society, the subject of our last year's lectures, and civil society, which we had proposed for our study this year. After attempting to define the relations of the family to the State, we have demonstrated the sacred character of the twofold element which constitutes the nation—Power, which is essentially divine, and the national soul, which is essentially religious. Considering, then, that nations, like families, are many, we asked ourselves whether there was not some bond by which they, in their turn, were united in a higher society; and after eliminating the political bond, as not adapted to this work, we have paused with admiration before the fellowship of nations constituted, at once, in the natural order, by the law of nations—in the supernatural order by the Catholic Church.

To-day the course of reasoning brings me into the presence of a fact not less frequent than terrible, which seems the negation of national fellowship. I mean War.

Pause, now, at the foot of this tree of death, which has taken so mighty and vast a growth in the world. Let us dig down to its roots, and find how deep they grow. Let us climb its huge trunk, and reach upon its branches those fatal but sometimes salutary fruits which the nations may pluck therefrom.

In other words, Gentlemen, I will inquire with you, in the first place, into the causes of war; and in the second place, I will attempt to penetrate its nature and results.

PART FIRST.—*The Origin of War.*

I. I will do for war, that law of death, what I have done for love, that law of life; I will look for its first root in the depth of the animal nature. They tell us, now-a-days, in the name of science falsely so called, that the historical origin of man was in the brute. Under every error there is hid a truth; and long before modern science, the Fathers of the Church had taught that man should contemplate in the lower races not only the diversified but faithful rough-drafts of his bodily organism, but the complete assemblage of the passions of his soul. It is not without reason that the Creator introduced man's appearance on the earth by the long preceding appearance of the brute. Through all the lapse of those "days" of Genesis, which undoubtedly were ages and myriads of ages, brute life was the necessary preface to human life. It was written then by the hand of God, and we are reading it to-day. Now, if I survey the series of those beings which might be called, in the language of Francis of Assisi, "our inferior brethren," everywhere among them I find war. In the air and on the earth, everywhere death-groans, blood- .

shed, lacerated flesh, and shattered bones. The silent depths of ocean hide no different scene. War, then, seems to be the very law of the relations of being. If I were to formulate this law, I should do it thus: Life is feeble and incapable of self-sustentation, and needs aliment; life has an overflowing fecundity, and needs a limit. God has appointed death to furnish both of these. Some simple-minded Christians suppose that, before the sin of Adam, the animals were free from every instinct of ferocity. St. Thomas Aquinas answered all such long ago. Discord between animals is not a consequence of sin, but a condition of nature. This is that fierce, cruel breath—at once destructive and conservative, conservative because destructive, and destructive because conservative—which breathes in the very vitals of life. It is not sin, but God, that does all this. It is he that has stretched the sway of death, and with death of war, from one end of creation to the other.

Weary, now, with this spectacle of horror—for it is horror, after all—let me lift my eyes toward that other world. . . . I have been looking upon the lower world. Let me look now into the world above, that world which reason suspects to exist, which experience has never reached, but of which revelation recounts the history—the world of spirits. An endless chain of bodily existences stretches down below me. Above me, how is it—since I am the microcosm, the centre and epitome of the world? May it not be that there is another chain of spiritual existences, individuals and races, richer still in their development?

Hail, angelic world! Thou, at least, shalt present the spectacle of peace! This is the world of truth: truth is the creator of order, and order is the creator of peace. Saint Augustine has defined peace to be the "tranquillity of order," *tranquillitas ordinis.* Here shall I find the tranquillity of order majestically poised in those regions of serenity and light.

Ah, no, Gentlemen, no! The historian of the world above tells us quite another tale. He shows us, if I might so express myself, the breath of the animal nature rising toward the sky, and discord breaking out in heaven. "I saw," says St. John the prophet, "and behold a great red dragon"* of the hue of blood. This is he of whom Jesus Christ declared that "he was a murderer from the beginning."† It is the father of death and the inventor of war. "And his tail drew the third part of the stars of heaven! .... And there was war in heaven. Michael and his angels fought against the dragon; and the dragon fought and his angels;" and Satan was vanquished and cast out into the earth. This is no mere conflict of ideas—ideas of truth in conflict with ideas of error. It is no mere conflict of hearts, the inspiration of great souls answering against the rebellion or defection of perverted ones. It is more than this: it is *force.* Men speak of "force and matter," as if they were correlatives. It is a just expression, force and matter; but here is another that is just too— "force and mind." In the mind of man, in the mind of angels, there is more than thought, more than feeling, more than volition : there is substantial energy— *force.* And when force meets force, there is war. It is not said of Satan that he was convinced, but that he was "cast out."‡

[Such is the *extra-human* origin of war. Father Hyacinthe deemed it needful to go so far back, in order to explain its human origin.]

* Revelation, xii. 3.   † John, viii. 14.
‡ Revelation, xii. 3-9.

II. I come now to man. "Man," says Pascal, "is neither angel nor brute;" but he is a sort of strange mixture—if I were not speaking of God's work, I would say, an odd mixture of brute and angel. In his lower nature I perceive the instincts of the brute. That conservative-destructive force which agitates the whole animal kingdom is to be perceived in the veins of man, and even in those regions of the soul which the scholastic philosophy has so well described, in which the "concupiscible appetite" and the "irascible appetite" are sustained each by the other, and are sometimes fused into one. Man, it is true, has received the gift of reason, to control, repress, direct his passions. But see how, bordering on one side on the passions of the brute, he borders, on the other side, on the pride of the angel. Cast out upon the earth, the fallen angel has come upon the cradle of mankind and flooded it with his venom. Thenceforth perverted, that reason which should have governed everything for good ends has governed everything for evil. Entering into alliance with gusty passions and with material forces, it has developed war to proportions which otherwise it would never have attained.

Man is pre-eminently the warrior of creation—as the Scripture calls him, "a mighty hunter before the Lord." The same Scripture likens his whole life on the earth to a warfare.

Fightings within himself! The brute and the angel wage within us that conflict of which every man is conscious, in which we escape the bondage of the senses only to fall an easy prey to pride. Fightings in the family! Husband divided against wife, and father against child, and a man's foes they of his own household. Cain leading his brother Abel into the field, and there rising up against him, and shedding for the first time that blood which the affrighted earth shall drink, and for which it shall never cease to cry for vengeance. Fightings between races, and through all society. In those early days of the world's infancy "there were giants in the earth," the "mighty men" of their time and the "men of renown;" and their outrages were washed away in the waters of the great flood, only to reappear in other forms on this globe, this field of everlasting battle.

[III. From the very nature of the origin of war, one might justly conclude that it is likely to be perpetual in the bosom of fallen humanity. The existence of war does not depend on circumstances external to human nature. It is not to be reckoned among those imperfections of society which may be expected to disappear in the progress of reason and morality. It is one of the permanent effects of original sin.]

Universal peace, proceeding from the indefinite development of human nature, and from what people call by a great name, used often without meaning—*Progress*—such universal peace is, then, a chimera. True, it is a chimera of noble minds and generous hearts; but they have not taken into their calculation either Christianity or facts.

Speak to me of the progress towards peace, of ideas, of morals, and even of the institutions of Christian society, tending to render the chances of war more and more difficult, and I can understand this language, and applaud it. I do not belong to that school of Catholics who make war to be a sort of divine ideal. War is the ideal of sin, as I have just been saying—the ideal of the brute and the devil. Peace, on the contrary, is the ideal of Christianity. But we do not reach our ideal on earth, nor even approach it except in so far as we follow the ways which lead to it. The Author of peace—we have just been celebrating the festival of his birth—we Christians, and perhaps you, rationalists, may have done the same, in the involuntary recollection of your childish days, and the magic of the songs of the Christmas night. "Unto us a child is born," cries Isaiah, "and the government shall be upon his shoulder, and his name shall be called the Prince of Peace."* Under his reign, the nations shall break their swords, and beat them into ploughshares; the garment rolled in blood shall be for burning and fuel of fire. Ah, Gentlemen, the prophet gives no promise that these wonders shall be wrought by the old humanity. On the contrary, they are promised through this new-born child, young as that eternity from whence he comes, and as that future whither he goes. "The Father of the Age to come," which shall be far other than the ages past, over his cradle the angels shall sing, "Glory to God in the highest, peace on earth to men of good will."† And over his opened sepulchre, in the splendor of his resurrection, himself, victor over death, the world, and hell, shall say to his disciples, "Be not afraid; my peace I leave with you."

PART SECOND.—*The Nature and Effects of War.*

[The nature of war being under consideration, Father Hyacinthe establishes, at the outset, a new application of that mysterious dualism which governs the created world, and especially the world as fallen. There are two sorts of war, pagan war and Christian war. Pagan war is force in the service of passion, from the transports of revenge to the calculations of ambition. Christian war is force in the service of right, whether in protection of one's own rights, or in the way of intervention in behalf of the rights of others.]

* Isaiah, ix. 6.   † Luke, II. 14.   Vulgate, "pax hominibus bonæ voluntatis."

I.—*Pagan War; or Force in the Service of Passion.*

I have wished to avoid the subject of universal empire. But it comes up again, to-day, at the heart of my subject, and I am compelled, now, to consider it.

Universal empire involves pagan war. Its instrument is the sword—the sword of conquest, which never says Enough, because it is wielded by the fiercest and the most cold-blooded of human passions, the passion for domination. Nebuchadnezzar, king of the Assyrians, having defeated in battle his powerful neighbor the king of the Medes, felt his heart lifted up in himself, and swore by his throne that he would extend his dominion far and wide. He summoned his councillors and his captains, and held with them, in his palace, what the Scripture has so well called "The mystery of his counsel."[*] A policy like his has full need of mystery. It shuns the light of day, and no wonder. For the secret of Nebuchadnezzar is no longer a secret. It has passed from empire to empire, from cabinet to cabinet, and it is to-day the object of the scorn and indignation of the whole world. "He declared that the thought of his heart was this: to subject the whole earth to his sway." The secret's out! Mark it: that proud but foolish thought—to rule the universe! He summons Holofernes, the captain of his host. "March," said he, "against the nations of the West, especially against those who have ventured to disobey my commandments. Seize their strong cities, subdue their kingdoms." Holofernes obeyed, and his innumerable hosts spread like locusts over the face of the earth. Everywhere they carried devastation and death, and the terror of Nebuchadnezzar king of the Assyrians. But

---

[*] Judith, ii. 2.

lo! in the midst of these nations of slaves, one of those petty States on which men had looked down with scorn, and in this petty State a little hamlet, hidden among the hills of Palestine, that had never heard of the splendors of the great principalities of Asia! In the home of her fathers, in sackcloth and ashes, a young widow was mourning her husband, and praying to her God. Judith rises in the name of her imperilled country. Armed with her chaste beauty and her God-given courage, she goes alone into the barbarian camp, and returns not till she brings in her woman's hands—I had almost said, her virgin hands—the tyrant's head, dripping with blood.

All honor to little Judea! What pity, if it had become a province of that Assyrian empire with which it was related by so many ties of origin and speech! Without Judea, we should be neither Frenchmen nor Christians, but only a fraction of the immense agglomeration of nations that made up the Roman empire.

All honor to the little States! They were constituted by the hand of God, and I hope in him that he will not suffer them to be destroyed. His providence presides in history, and has placed them between the great States as the negation of universal empire, the pacific obstacle to the shocks of their power, the plots of their ambition.

The little States! They are the representatives of right in its most affecting form—right unarmed and defenceless.

The little States! They are the radiating centres of the most splendid civilization, from the cities of ancient Greece, that gave us an Æschylus and a Sophocles, an Aristides and a Plato, down to those republics of modern Italy to which we owe the Revival of Learning.

[This dream of universal empire, which made Alexander weep to think that the world had limits, while his ambition had none, has taken, in later times, another form.]

We know the earth better now. We know that its extent is too vast to submit to any single empire. But there is a fancy, now-a-days, for dividing it into vast zones, each of which represents a world. There is the Sclavonic world, the Germanic world, the American world, not to mention others. Now, within the limits of each of these worlds, the effort is made to consolidate the peoples by violently tearing asunder the sacred bonds of history and treaties. Men appeal to the natural right of the race, and, if need be, to a higher mission, mysterious as fate. And while they are trying to fuse together kingdoms and nations in the crucibles of this novel alchemy, our pseudo-philosophers stand by and cry out, Progress!

I say it is going backward toward the ages of barbarism. I come back to my book, my inspired Bible. Daniel saw them—these giant empires—both in prophecy and in history, and, like Saint Peter in his trance, he beheld them in the form of beasts. "In the first year of Belshazzar king of Babylon, Daniel had a dream, and visions of his head upon his bed; and he wrote the dream, and told the sum of the matters."* He saw mankind under its most natural image, a vast and surging sea, and darkness was upon the face of it; "and, behold, the four winds of heaven were in strife upon the great sea." The prophet watched the storm, and presently there emerged from the billows four monstrous beasts. The first was like a lion, and had wings, whereby its wrath might rage from end to end of the earth with the swiftness of an eagle. Another was like

* Daniel, vii. 1.

a leopard; it had four heads, and the four quarters of the world bowed down before it. Then came the northern bear, its jaws armed with a triple row of teeth, and Daniel heard a voice saying, "Arise, devour much flesh." And while the bear rose up to its hideous banquet, there appeared behind it another monster, more terrible and strange than all the rest. Its teeth and claws were of iron. It did not eat, but mangled, and when it had mangled with its bloody jaws, it stamped the residue with its feet. Upon its brow it wore an evergrowing horn, the type of brute force. And this horn, the seat, likewise, of its spiritual pride, had eyes like the eyes of man, and a blaspheming mouth speaking great things against righteousness and against God.

Cease! cease, ye gloomy visions! I too have beheld you with my own eyes, not in prophecy, but in history.

II. *Christian War, or Force in the Service of Right.*

"I beheld," continues Daniel (and this was written ages before the coming of Jesus Christ), "I beheld in the night-vision, and behold with the clouds of heaven came one like the Son of man, and drew near to the Ancient of Days. And to him were given dominion and glory and a kingdom, that all people, nations, and languages should serve him; whose dominion is an everlasting dominion, which shall not pass away, and his kingdom that which shall not be destroyed."* On the ruins of those empires of violence, the Redeemer has come to plant this new empire, under which all nations, maintaining their independence, shall be, nevertheless, one people of God. This is Christian civilization, or, to use a more old-fashioned expression, this is *Christen-*

* Daniel, vii. 13, 14.

dom—an empire peaceful in its nature, since it is not propagated by the sword, but which puts on its warrior's armor whenever it is needful to defend itself against its enemies. The Son of man is the Prince of peace; but yet, as the prophets beheld him, there went forth from between his teeth a two-edged sword.

[It is this material sword which God has not committed to the peaceful hands of the chiefs of his Church, but which he has intrusted to the civil powers—empires or republics. The only mission of this sword is to defend righteousness against violent aggression. Father Hyacinthe inquires why it is spoken of as a sword with two edges.]

It is because there are two sorts of attack upon Christian civilization—two forms of barbarism which menace it from without and from within.

Every unjust aggression on the frontiers of a nation is an act of barbarism. The nation, then, in the person of those who represent and govern it, must have power to draw the sword and smite the barbarian. The rights of individuals may sometimes stand defenceless under the oppression of the strong, and then it is that there remains for justice its sublimest triumph—martyrdom. Not so with the rights of States. For them it would not be moral heroism, it would be a crime as well as a disgrace, to turn the left cheek when smitten on the right. A great Italian patriot has said: " Independence is to nations what modesty is to women. What are all the other virtues worth, when this is wanting?"*

* * * * * * *

Within, there is another form of barbarism. Not that of the nation. The nation has no need to be de-

* Cesar Balbo, " Les Esperances de l'Italie."

fended against itself. It is both conservative and liberal. Enthroned at all its firesides, there is but one thing which it more abhors than foreign war, and that is civil war. But there have been in every age, and they especially abound in evil times, a minority having no concern with interests or duties, and who, powerless in the world of thought, are always ready to appeal to violence. With this internal barbarism, so long as it makes no aggressions, the sword has nothing to do. It amounts to a principle with all free nations, that armed force is not to interfere in matters of internal police; and among our neighbors, whose example I have had such frequent occasion to cite, the constable carries for his sole but sufficient badge of authority the wand of the law. But when rebellion flies to arms, then the nation, its prince at its head, must draw against it that sword of which the apostle says that "the Power beareth not the sword in vain, for he is the minister of God to execute wrath on him that doeth evil."*

[Such is the essentially defensive character of that Christian war, in which force is exclusively at the service of right. From this, Father Hyacinthe infers the dignity of the soldier's profession, and the grandeur of his mission in modern civilization. He especially honored, in the army, that sentiment of hierarchy and discipline which tends, of late, to grow weaker in the rest of the nation.]

I have never honored insult and insurrection with the name of liberty. Liberty, in my view, is the dignity of that man who bows to the authority of his own conscience, and consequently to the law and the magistrate. No one is free until he has learned how to obey. Now this grand spirit of obedience is becoming lost among us, and we need the army to preserve it to

* Romans, xiii. 4.

us. It is not a coffle of slaves, Gentlemen. These are soldiers—French soldiers. They had a pretorian guard at Rome: in France we have never had other than soldiers—soldiers who find, in the sword by their side, in the flag above their head, the double lesson of obedience and of honest pride.

[In speaking of the nature of war, Father Hyacinthe only very slightly indicated its effects. These, he said, would of themselves require an entire discourse. The immediate effects of it are always destructive; so that it must always be a maxim of national wisdom, "He who makes two blades of grass grow where only one grew before, has done more for mankind than the victor of a hundred battles." And yet Providence, accustomed to bring good out of evil, has often placed in war the principle of the moral regeneration of society.]

These are the terrible but incontestable benefits which, in conclusion, I would indicate in a single word. But, great God! what shall I say? There are hours in the life of nations when peace becomes a peril and almost a scourge. Wealth is too often a fatal thing to individuals, not because it is an evil,—on the contrary, it is a great good; but perverse man turns even good into a curse, especially when this good smiles upon his passions. Thus divine Wisdom has said, "Blessed are the poor! How hard is it for a rich man to enter the kingdom of heaven!" Peace, too, is a good yet more excellent, and yet when nations abuse it, it may be as fatal to them as wealth to the individual. Peace, indeed, develops wealth, and sets it circulating through the body of society. Then, with wealth, it develops luxury, in private life as well as public, and especially among women, with whom it puts on its most seductive and corrupting character. And all the time, as in a splendid but infected sepulchre, the morals of the people go on decaying in this terrible calm—and with them its understanding perishes also. I have sometimes compared the sophist and the harlot: I must never do it again in this pulpit, if I have any regard for rhetoric. But I don't care for rhetoric; I am resolved to lay bare the wounds which society so obstinately hides. Yes; while luxury is consuming a nation's vitals, while in the midst of increasing dissoluteness the harlots lift their shameless heads on every side, like worms upon the corpse on which they feed, there rises up another brood of corruption and death, which attacks, not the heart, but the brain—it is the sophists, corrupters at once of the public reason and of the language which is its organ. They make their attack in succession on the greatest words of that language—liberty, progress, civilization, morality, and even God; and in these sacred vessels of speech, in place of the perfume of the truth, they leave a deadly poison. They make it their business to pervert all just ideas and supplant them by vague and unreal abstractions. Then, amid these phantoms that they are chasing in the void, and embracing in the sweet delusion of a dream, as Orpheus embraced Eurydice at the gates of hell, these demented souls keep crying out, "Facts! facts! leave theories to the old folks! give us facts and realities!"

Facts, forsooth! Well, here they are! The enemy at our gates, our honor insulted, our independence menaced! If nothing less than this will serve to save us from the toils of those who would drag us down to ruin, then God will grant us this, for he loves us and will save us from ourselves. Facts! Here are facts which sober us from our intoxication with abstractions, and bring back the sense of reality—war! victory or death! The flag of France torn with shot, stained with blood, drooping in glorious tatters, but never receding! The women of France rising indignant behind their husbands and their sons, and driving before the scourge of their righteous anger and disgust this rabble-rout of harlots and sophists! Make way there for the Sister of Charity, that comes to tend the wounded on the battle-field! Make way for the Catholic priest, till now neglected and despised, sneered at as a man of the past, a man of foreign sympathies, when all the time he is the nation's own man, for the present and the past alike: he is at hand now with the consolations of religion, comforting in his arms, cherishing with tears and kisses those who are dying with no mother by their side.

As those days draw nigh, as in the days of Israel's calamity, men cry, Peace! peace! But the Lord, perhaps, has said War! The monarchs go about one to another calling each other Brother, and then, as if they doubted of it, saying it over again. The peoples do but make echo to their kings. From the coasts of the Atlantic to the shores of the Mediterranean, interests in coalition protest against war, now by the dull silence of business, now by the noisy complaints of working-men. The talking men and the writing men come to the support of business interests in the name of ideas, and once more the whole world is crying Peace! And yet, as under some overhanging storm, we seem to feel the thunder in the air, so the people vaguely perceive in their atmosphere that terrible gathering of electricity which Jesus Christ has spoken of as "rumors of wars."

Son of Bethlehem! Father of the Age to come! Prince of peace! O grant us that peace which is peace indeed! Scatter these rumors of wars, save each nation by itself, regenerate France by her own children! So grand she is, even yet; so peaceful and so prosperous she might be, if only left to her own true instincts!

But if it is too late—great God, if, in thy wisdom, thou hast otherwise decided, then bring back to us, upon the battle-field, that faith which on the battle-field we first received; that faith of Tolbiac which made us great, but which it is sought to ravish from us. Pour out in war the blood of our young men, too precious to dry up in sterility, or be corrupted in the pleasures of an unworthy peace. Leap from the scabbard, thou sword of the Lord and of France, *gladius Domini et Gedeonis*, and do thy work! Do it speedily, and do it to the end!

And then, "O thou sword of the Lord, put up thyself into thy scabbard: rest, and be still!"*

* Jeremiah, xlvii. 6.

LECTURE SIXTH.

January 5, 1868.

CIVILIZATION.

My Lord Archbishop, and Gentlemen: The nations constitute among themselves a higher commonwealth so intimate and necessary, that war itself, with all its discords and its horrors, does not suffice to destroy it. But have they not also some work to do in common, the fruit of the development of each, and the mutual relations of all? To put this question is to answer it; and that with the one word Civilization.

It is a vague word, I know, like all words that denote general ideas. It is subject, consequently, to the most diverse interpretations; often, alas! to the most mischievous perversions. But is this a reason why we should give up using it? Because it is a pleasure to feeble or perverse minds to wither everything they touch, must we leave them free to deflower a language and corrupt at will its noblest words and its most legitimate ideas? I think not, Gentlemen; and that is the reason why I mean to hold on by that word *civilization,* and why I undertake to define it.

Civilization seems to me to be in the body politic what health is to the natural body—the result of a practical harmony between the organic functions and the laws of life. For the same reason, barbarism seems to me like a morbid state, in which the constitutional principles of the social system are habitually neglected and violated. I will define civilization, then, as the state of a nation whose activity, regulated by justice, is developed in the direction of material and moral welfare; or, in other words, as the practice of virtuous and prosperous nations.

Civilization is both complex and multiform—complex, because it includes many elements; multiform, because it is realized in many different ways. So that, from the start, we reject that invariable mould which a certain school of publicists would fain impose on all the races of mankind. One single form could not possibly fit all lands and all ages, nor, in the same land and age, all classes of society. In Europe, we have no exclusive and inaccessible castes, but we have, and always shall have, classes.

Now I distinguish between two leading forms of civilization, which I shall take as the heads of this discourse—one answering to the wants of the great majority of men, embracing the primitive and indispensable elements of public order, and forming the vast basis of the social pyramid; the other, concentrating in the hands of the comparatively few what I shall speak of as the accessory forces of civilization, and displaying at the summit of the social edifice a magnificence which, though the property of the few, redounds none the less to the advantage and the honor of all.

PART FIRST.—*The Essential Laws of Civilization*

[Father Hyacinthe proves that, in its primitive and essential form, civilization results from the fulfilment of three great laws: the law of love in the family, the law of labor in the field, the law of prayer in the temple.]

I. *The Law of Love in the Family.*

I have spoken before now about love in the family—quite too much about it, some people say. I am only sorry that I have not said more. To exhibit the indissoluble union between love and the family is the noblest and most needed task that any earnest man, and especially any priest, can set himself. For my part, I have never been able to put myself into the position of those theologians, with neither heart nor genius, who ignore this great sentiment of the human soul, and are afraid, apparently, to pollute their lips by uttering its name. I make bold to declare that it is such men as these who have unconsciously prepared the way for the dynasty of those conscienceless writers who, separating, after their fashion, passion from duty, extol love without comprehending its true dignity, and inflict upon it that supreme outrage of confounding it with caprice and lust. Except when it fixes its undivided gaze on heaven, and becomes virginity, love cannot blossom, save in the sanctuary of home, with that twofold bloom, so beautiful and yet so serious and holy—marriage and parentage.

However, I have no occasion, just now, to recur to this important subject. I will only observe, that in all prosperous nations public life is subordinate to private life. This is true not only in this sense, that the State, having for its mission to protect the rights of the family, holds toward it the relation of means to end, and that the means is necessarily subordinate to the end; but in this higher sense, that the citizens themselves concentrate in their homes the noblest of their activities, convinced that, as the best and worthiest service to humanity is attained by serving it in one's own country, so one may best serve and love his country in his family. There, most of all, is played the drama of human life, intense and ravishing as the best passions of the heart, grave as duty, active as the pursuit of interest (which is itself a duty), calm and recollected as study and prayer. It is, therefore, to impel any people in a direction full of falsehood and peril, to hold exclusively, or even principally, before it the prospects of the political career. Doubtless the life of a great nation is at the polls and in the legislature, but far more than this, it is at the fireside. Where shall we find philosophers to teach us this—authors and artists to depict it—where, above all, the men to live it? Ah! look beyond the Alps, at our little neighbor, Switzerland, home of toilsome industry and of the household, of simple, honest, happy life!—home, too, of free, traditional democracy! And here, poor French democracy, despising the family, despising religion, here thou art lying yet, after eighty years, crying, helpless, in thy bloody swaddling clothes!

II. *The Law of Labor in the Field.*

[Coming to this law of labor, so closely related to the law of the family, Father Hyacinthe remarked that it is peculiar to the human race. Generally speaking, the brute, left to himself, does no labor; while man from his very creation was under the glorious necessity of work. "The Lord God placed him in the garden of Eden to dress it and to keep it."* By the great mass of men this toil is exercised by the hands and upon matter, and, more particularly still, in the tillage of the ground. "In the sweat of his face, he is to eat bread."†]

Agriculture, then, is one of the chief laws of civilization. And considering that at this very hour while I

* Genesis, ii. 15. † Ibid., iii. 19.

am speaking, a national ceremony is taking place in honor of it,* I may be allowed to insist upon its importance, so often overlooked. I would never separate the interests of religion from those of my own country. I know there are those who consider this combination dangerous, or at least unsuitable. To me, it is the simple duty of a Christian and a citizen.

Agriculture, I say, is the chief and primitive element of civilization; and this for three reasons. First, because by effecting the transition from nomadic to settled life, it becomes the starting-point of civil society. Secondly, because it yields the great product of civilization in the material order, the necessary basis of the spiritual order—bread. Finally, because it holds the population to their most appropriate residence, out of the city, and in the country.

1. Agriculture the starting-point of civil society.

Before the tillage of the earth commences, men live in wandering tribes of hunters, or more commonly shepherds. These are not savages, as I have already shown. We have dwelt with admiration on their way of living on the lofty table-lands of Asia, the region of rich pasturage, as if we looked upon it in the pages of Genesis, under the tents of Abraham and Isaac and Jacob. But neither are they civilized, in the sense in which we are now using the word, for they have no civil organization. It is the tillage of the earth which halts the wanderer, and holds him to the meadow, the wood, the valley, by whose riches or beauty he has been charmed. He pitches his tent, plants his landmarks, and establishes between himself and the soil that settled alliance of which are born at once two great, and in their turn pro-

---

* The distribution of prizes for agriculture at the Universal Exposition of 1867.

lific facts,—the organization of property, and the organization of labor. Property existed before; the family owned its tent and all it contained. Labor also existed before; the shepherds tended their flocks. But neither labor nor property were organized. From the hour this organization begins, it takes cognizance of interests, and so of rights. For it is the peculiar glory of man, that for him, underneath every interest, there lies a right. From this coming together of all interests and all rights, there grows up the necessity, more and more keenly felt, of a common arbiter, a central sovereign power, in a word, of civil society.

2. Agriculture the bread-producing power.

Modern science analyzes bread, and shows us marvellous things; but it has not seen nor told the half.[*] But it has shown us how the corn, that foster-father of nations, goes seeking through the soil, by potent and infallible instinct, the imperceptible traces of the elements necessary for our bodies,—the phosphorus, for example, essential to our bones; and then concentrates it into the rich and generous grain,—grain, the earth's milk for man, as milk is the mother's bread for her child—the royal aliment of the civilized nations! I am well aware that it is not such universally, but it is among the causes which have contributed to place us of Occidental Christendom in the highest grade of civilization.

Bread, the food of the body, is in one sense the food of the soul. Boast yourselves as you may, ye men of thought; for all that, your intellect would go out into nothingness but for the blood flowing to the brain, like oil in the lamp, actually keeping alive that flame of

---

[*] See the remarkable "*Rapport sur les commerces du blé, de la farine et du pain,*" by *M. Le Play. Quarto; Paris,* 1860.

thought which illuminates and warms the world, if, alas! it do not destroy it. It is from bread that the blood derives its best juices, so that the development of genius as well as of wealth is traceable to its origin in a grain of wheat.

All life is in the bread—material life, as in its substance; intellectual life, as in its instrument; religious life, as in its symbol. And to behold the crowning glory of the bread, we must follow it to the Catholic altar, where, in the hands of Christ, by the most amazing of all mysteries, it becomes the eternal food of the soul, and the august centre of the religion of the human race—"the bread of God, which giveth life unto the world."*

3. Agriculture as holding civilization to the arena of its best achievements—country life.

I have no disposition to be unjust toward the city. I would not speak of cities, with the poet, as "the sties of nations."† And I do not look, with him, for their disappearance in the course of time. Whatever the vice and wretchedness which they hide, or which they engender, cities are the necessary and glorious centres of national life. But they are exceptional centres. The real scene prepared by Providence for the social activities of man, is not in the city, but in the country. There, are gathered, with a sort of prodigality, the conditions most favorable to the health, both of body and of soul. There, the laboring population realize most readily the prolific wedlock of happiness and virtue; while the upper classes, themselves kept free from corruption, find opportunity of exercising, on a vast scale, that benign influence of fortune and education which should be their highest delight, as it is their holiest

* John, vi. 33.   † M. de Lamartine.

duty. The absenteeism of the rich, forerunner of the absenteeism of the peasantry, was the beginning of our plagues. Their only remedy will be to revive, under such new forms as may suit the present state of society, the traditions of the cottage and the manor-house. We shall never be effectually decentralized, until this conviction is carried into the minds, and still more into the hearts of men. The best dwelling-place for man is not in capitals, nor even in provincial cities, but in the country. Whenever I see, in any nation, the setting of a current against nature, the tide of population running in a fatal direction, the blood of the body politic all determining toward the head, I look with dread for the result. I have no applause for these factitious splendors, and I cry out, like Henry III., in the presence of what was, even then, the overgrown metropolis, that "Paris is too big a head for France to carry."

III. *The Law of Prayer in the Temple.*

The law of the family and the law of labor yield their rich delights only at cost of many sacrifices. And to these, men would not long submit, but for the help of religion. The law of prayer, binding in itself, is more binding in view of these two other laws, the fulfilment of which it secures.

I like facts; especially the sort of facts in which we find at once poetry, morality, and utility. Permit me, then, to refer once more to the example of that little population of Basques, on whose frontiers I passed my childhood. Thanks to their isolated dwellings, their old traditionary freedom, larger and more practical than our modern liberties, thanks especially to their inherited morality and religion, the Basques, in a mountain country, little suited for tillage, have realized the ideal of rural life. Under that Biscayan sky, the murkiest sky of Spain, they present the rare spectacle of a contented and happy people, disdaining wealth, but never knowing poverty. So perfect is the security which prevails among them, that the cattle and crops lie in the fields without fear of robbers, being (as some one finely says) under guard of the Eighth Commandment.

[Father Hyacinthe insisted at length on the observance of the Lord's Day, as the realization of the social law of prayer. The Lord's Day kept by the country-people in worship and festivity, in the double sanctuary of church and home, is the badge of civilization. On the contrary, in our great cities, the Sabbath violated with labor and blasphemy, and the Monday given over to drunken festivity, are symptoms of the most abject barbarism.]

I cannot refrain, here, from calling your attention to a contrast which is, at the same time, a harmony. This city, which has so many claims to be called illustrious, which, in so many respects, is at the head of the civilized world, has always acknowledged as its patron saint a humble country-girl, the shepherdess Genevieve. Through all the vicissitudes of the centuries, the heart of Paris has been constant to her; and even now, each day, about her shrine, the high and the lowly come together with common devotion and a common trust. They remember how she brought the boats up the Seine to feed Paris in the famine; how, with prophetic instinct, she distinguished among the incoming torrents of the barbarians, those that could do nothing but destroy from those that might restore; how, by the puissance of her prayer, she drove back the Huns, with Attila, toward Asia, and brought back the Franks, with Clovis, to baptism and civilization. She who wrought these mighty works was but a country-girl, but she was not a barbarian; and it is most just and fit that she presides at Paris over the destinies of France and civilization.

Part Second.—*The Higher Civilization.*

[Father Hyacinthe proposed to show three things: the fact of a higher civilization; the right of such a civilization to exist; the dangers attending it.]

I. *The Fact of a Higher Civilization.*

The two laws of the family and of worship are the same at the bottom of society and at the top. Not so with the law of labor. Labor is not wholly for the hands. There comes a day when, entering on the vast fields of mind, it seeks to till them, in their turn, and sow them with the seed of science. Science, at that stage of development at which it is worthy of the name, is not an absolute necessity of human nature. If man knows his own soul and God, love and duty, labor and death, he knows the answer to those supreme questions which are put to him by consciousness within and by the world without. But none the less is science the indispensable luxury of great civilizations. It is developed in two principal directions, the contemplative and the active.

Contemplative science—what is there that it has not included in its scope? It has scrutinized the invisible, weighed the imponderable, decomposed the molecule, in the laboratories of its physics and its chemistry. Queen of the inorganic world, it is extending its conquests, day by day, by means of physiology, into the organic world; and, laying hands upon life itself in the currents of blood which it interrogates and directs at will, it seeks to penetrate those awful secrets which we have been carrying about with us in our own bodies, without daring to explore them. Its realm extends even to higher spheres than this. It takes to itself the name of philosophy, and hovers aloft in the regions of the soul, and above the soul it studies the ideas which enlighten it, and, far above the ideas, God who gives them light. Yes! to start from the atom, to go mounting upward, by the blood, by the ideas, by God himself, up to the very topmost height of things, never pausing until, like the dazed eagle, it hangs poised with eye fixed upon the sun—this is the career of science! Ah! I could lift up a lamentation that should not be comforted, were humanity to be bereft of these sublime audacities, of the ravishment of these prolific joys!

And yet this is not all. Science, as I have just hinted, is a prolific mother. She cannot remain cloistered in the sanctuary of contemplation, like a virgin in her calm and luminous beauty. She comes back into the sphere of material activity; she is wedded to productive toil, and they are the parents of power and riches. Into the hands of the laborer from the plough she puts implements and methods that are akin to the miraculous, and bids him Go, subdue the world, and transform it. And—as in these Titanic wars that are led by genius and waited on by fortune, each day is marked by some resplendent victory—so discovery succeeds discovery, each surpassing that which went before, and science applied by industry impels society from triumph on to triumph, toward a future which they do but just dimly descry, and the prospect of which at once enraptures and dismays.

And then over the stalwart and naked shoulders of

this positive civilization which controls and operates material forces, lo! Art draws nigh to fling its starry and imperial robe—all the glories of painting, sculpture, and architecture—all the harmonies of music and of poetry, falling from heaven, like a transfiguration, upon the stir and din of human toil.

II. *The Right of the Higher Civilization to Exist.*

[This civilization is not only a fact, but a right and a duty—the right of man's royalty over nature—the duty of God's vicegerent over the creation. It is the fulfilment of the primitive command, "Be fruitful and multiply, and replenish the earth and subdue it."*

Father Hyacinthe remarked that in order to facilitate the fulfilment of this command by Christian nations, divine Providence has developed in them the faculty of production and that of abstraction to a degree utterly unknown to pagan society.

That civilization which is founded on self-denial and renunciation of the world, has achieved the highest success, in private and public fortune. It is by seeking, first and exclusively, the kingdom of God and his righteousness, that man has been brought into possession of the world.

As to the faculty of abstraction, in which science properly so called originates, it is undoubtedly an appanage of the European race. But it has received its full development only under the influence of Christianity. How vast the difference between the heathen and the Christian reason!—between the scientific genius of ancient Greece, and that of the doctors of the Church, and of the Christian philosophers!]

III. *The Dangers of the Higher Civilization.*

[The experience of every age assures us that nations are but too easily drawn into the abuse of wealth and science; or rather that such abuses are inevitable, in the absence of an energetic and sustained struggle against the effects of original sin. From these abuses, when they become multiplied, results that twofold cor-

* Genesis, 1. 28.

ruption to which Father Hyacinthe has already animadverted, and which is growing upon us more and more—the corruption of morals, and the corruption of the reason itself.]

We had in France, at the beginning of this century, a great school of Transcendental philosophy, which, unhappily incomplete on some points, erroneous on others, is none the less the lasting honor of a country of which it failed to be the salvation. It relegated to the eighteenth century those materialist or simply sensualist doctrines the wretched and unwholesome traditions of which it refused to propagate, so that no one would have guessed, at that time, how speedily they would be coming back upon us. But victorious over materialism, inheriting, in part at least, the traditions of Plato, it thought itself in a position to dispense with the Christian revelation. It ignored the realities of the moral and religious life, and perverting ideas as others had perverted facts, it left behind it unfaithful, and yet perhaps logical disciples, who returned, by paths which itself had opened for them, to this very skepticism and materialism, the disgrace of which does, at this hour, weigh heavier than ever on the mind of France. A hideous intellectual barbarism, for which, for my part, I blush before Europe, and more yet before the future, and against which I can never protest often enough nor forcibly enough! It is not only the divine Word made flesh whose history and doctrine they blaspheme; it is the human Word itself that they would smother in those first lights which preside at once over the reason of philosophers and the common sense of the people. God is no longer a personal being. Under that conception he served to supply the craving of former ages. To-day he is an idea of the mind, a law of the universe, an abstraction. Free agency is a hallucination of the consciousness:

man is not free, even when he thinks himself so, for he always acts under the fatal pressure of motives. The difference between right and wrong varies with individuals as well as with periods and climates; it depends upon the varying points of view at which we stand, and in fact is nothing but an optical illusion!

I pause before these pernicious steeps, down which, from the very height of civilization, a nation, at least the upper classes of a nation, may go plunging into a barbarism infinitely deeper and more hopeless than that of rude and simple nations.

O, better far the peasantry, or (as our Democracy in its lofty and insolent language affects to call them), the "ignorant country-folks!" To them I turn in search of that the loss of which nothing can make good—the divine gift of common sense and good morals!

[From the perils of the higher civilization, Father Hyacinthe draws an important and unanticipated conclusion—that religion is even more needful to the rich than to the poor; to the great than to the masses.

Religion, furthermore, is not only the conservative force in human society in its present condition; still more is it the prophecy of its future. Man is a being too full of mysteries to end his career with the achievements of this earthly existence. Civilization is the expression of an ideal too grand to be realized, completely and absolutely, short of the commonwealth of eternity. This ultimate condition of things is that of which Cicero had a presentiment, when he declared "this universal world one general commonwealth of gods and men." *Universus hic mundus una civitas communis deorum atque hominum.** It is that which the prophets have contemplated under the image of the new Jerusalem, city of God, beginning on the earth, but completed only in heaven. "Behold the tabernacle of God with men, and he will dwell with them, and they shall be his people, and God himself shall be with them, and be their God."†]

* De Legibus, i., vii. † Revelation, xxi. 3.

The expectation of this highest life is expressed in one of the noblest and most misapprehended institutions of the Catholic church. Now that I have contemplated civilization under its various forms, suffer me to disengage from my poor person the sublimity of the monastic state, and to greet in the true monk, not some dead fossil of the unreturning past, but the boldest and most farsighted forerunner of the ultimate future. He is the man who, without despising what there is of grand and noble in this world, loving it, on the contrary, and keeping heart of hope for all its interests, warms with enthusiasm for a loftier form of goodness that is yet to come, but which is brought nigh to him by faith. He looks far beyond these most solid realities, to the boldest and most splendid Utopias, and ever, as humanity grows impatient of its voyage, and longs to land ere it has reached the port, he seems to point forward to some invisible shore, and say, "Not yet! not yet!"

In the life of Saint Benedict written by Saint Gregory the Great—historian worthy of his hero—it is reported that one night, just before the hour of those holy hymns which exhale from the cloister in the midst of silence and darkness, the man of God was gazing upon heaven through the window of his cell. A mystical light shone round about him, and the whole world was brought before him, as if it had been gathered up into one ray of sunlight. "He saw it," says the inscription which is read to this day in the tower in which he dwelt on Monte Cassino, "he saw it, and scorned it." *Inspexit et despexit.* This world which was his handiwork—his, the patriarch of the Monks of the West, patriarch I might say of European civilization—when he saw it lifted clear of the obscurities of time, into the light of the everlasting Sun, how petty and poor a world he found it!

Gentlemen, let us act like him. We are about to separate for one year more; let us pledge each other that we will toil with more intelligence and devotion than ever at the task of civilization in Europe, and first of all in France. To this let us apply our strength. On this let us expend our days and nights! But, in proportion as we shall accomplish this work, let us contemplate it in a light that comes from higher than itself, and higher than ourselves, in the divine radiance of the future. "*Inspexit et despexit.*" Let us love it as being the forerunner of the Future; let us scorn it as that which the Future shall so far excel.

SERMON

ON THE OCCASION OF THE PROFESSION OF CATHOLIC FAITH, AND THE FIRST COMMUNION, OF A CONVERTED PROTESTANT AMERICAN LADY.

I will sing of the mercies of the Lord forever."—PSALM lxxxix. 1.

MY SISTER IN JESUS CHRIST: It is from you that I have received the text and the subject of this exhortation. Overflowing with gratitude to Him who has called you out of darkness into his marvellous light, you have asked me to forget this audience, to think only of yourself and God, and to speak only of his loving-kindness which has been manifested in every event of your life. I consent to your request; and considering your life in the three divisions by which time is measured, in simple truth and the devout confidence of an overflowing heart, I will endeavor to speak of the designs of God in your past, your present, and your future. The history of Christian souls is the most wonderful and yet the most occult of all histories. The outward events which agitate society have their inner meaning and ultimate reason only in this; and when we shall come to read it in its completeness in the book of life, in the light of eternity, we shall find in it the irrefutable justification of the providence of God over human affairs, and the true title of the nobility of our race, in the blood and the mercy of Christ. "We shall sing of the mercies of the Lord forever."

I. And first, Madam, what are these mercies of your past life? And, that we may understand it better, what have you been, yourself, hitherto? I feel some embarrassment in answering my question. Born, as you were, in the midst of heresy, you were no heretic. No, thank God, you were no heretic, and nothing shall force me to apply to you that cruel—that justly cruel name, against which all my knowledge of your past makes protest. Saint Augustine, one of the most exact and rigid of the teachers of Christian antiquity, refuses, in more than one of his works, to include among heretics those who, born without the visible pale of the Catholic Church, have kept the sincere love of truth in their hearts, and are ready to follow it in all its manifestations and requirements.* What constitutes heresy is that spirit of pride, of revolt and schism which broke out in heaven when Satan, dividing the angels of light, tried to reconstruct, in his own fashion, the everlasting truth of God, and to remodel God's work in the world: it is the wrathful breath of this archangel's nostrils with which he would inspire those who, in like malignant spirit, should carry on his work from age to age. Meek and lowly of heart, you have never been inspired by that spirit. You were not, then, a heretic.

But what were you, then? I was talking one day with one of your most distinguished fellow-countrymen, a Protestant by birth, now a Catholic and a priest;† and under the impulse of that earnest inquisitiveness

---

* "Qui sententiam suam, quamvis falsam atque perversam, nulla pertinaci animositate defendunt, præsertim quam non audacia præsumptionis suæ pepererunt, sed a seductis atque in errorem lapsis parentibus acceperunt, quærunt autem cauta sollicitudine veritatem, corrigi parati, dum invenerint, nequaquam sunt inter hæreticos reputandi."—*Letter XLIII., Edition of the Benedictines of Saint Maur.*

† The Reverend Father Hecker, founder and Superior of the Congregation of Saint Paul.

which the history of souls always awakens in me, I asked him this same question, "What were you?" "I did not belong to any Protestant communion," he replied; "I was baptized in the church of my parents, but I never shared their faith." "Were you a Rationalist, then?" I said. "No," he smilingly answered; "in the United States we know nothing of that mental malady of the Europeans." I blushed, and was silent a moment, and then begged for an explanation, when he made me this grand reply: "I was a natural man, seeking the truth with my whole mind and heart."

Now, Madam, this is just what you were: a noble womanly nature, seeking the truth in love, and love in the truth; more than that, you were a Christian—yes, a Catholic.

There is a fundamental distinction, without which it is not possible to deal justly by the communions separated from the Catholic Church and the members of those communions. Every religious system contains within itself two opposite elements: the negative element, which makes it a schism, and most commonly a heresy; and the positive element, which preserves for it a greater or less share in the ancient heritage of Christianity. Not only distinct but hostile, they are very near to each other, even in their conflicts: darkness and light, life and death, mingle without being confounded, and there results from it all what I would call the deep and intricate mystery of the life of error. For my part, I do not render to error the undeserved honor of supposing it able to live of its own life, breathe by its own breath, and nourish with its own substance souls which are not without virtues, and nations not without greatness!

Protestantism, as such, is that negative element which

you have renounced, and to which, with the Catholic Church, you have said, Anathema. But Protestantism has not been the only thing in your past religious life: by the side of its negations have been its affirmations, and, like a savory fruit enclosed in a bitter husk, you have been in possession of Christianity from your cradle.

Before coming to us, you were a Christian by baptism validly received; and when the hand of the minister sprinkled the water on your brow with those words of eternal life, "I baptize thee in the name of the Father, and of the Son, and of the Holy Ghost," it was Jesus Christ himself who baptized you. "The hand is nothing," says Saint Augustine; "be it Peter's or Paul's, the hand is nothing—it is Christ that baptizes." It was Christ who betrothed you, who received your faith and pledged to you his own. The depth of your moral nature, that sacred part of noble souls which instinctively shrinks from error, the Word has consecrated to himself, that he "might present it to himself as a chaste virgin,"* reserving it for heaven.

You were a Christian, also, by the Gospel, as well as by baptism. The Bible was the book of your childhood, and you learned from it the secrets of this divine faith which belongs to every age, because it comes from eternity, with the accents of that Anglo-Saxon tongue which belongs to every land, because it prevails throughout the world by virtue of its civilizing force. The free exercise of private judgment, under the spirit of which you have grown up, is, doubtless, the source of numberless errors; but—thank God again for this—besides the Protestant principle, there is also the Christian principle among Protestants; besides private judgment,

* 2 Corinthians, xi. 2.

there is the action of the supernatural grace received in baptism, and of that mysterious influence of which Saint Paul speaks when he says, "We have the mind of Christ,"* and of which Saint John said, "Ye have an unction from the Holy One, and ye know all things."† When we read over again together that Gospel which separated our ancestors, I was pleasantly surprised, at every page, to find that we understood it in the same sense, and that, consequently, when you read it outside of the Church, you did not read it without the spirit of the Church.

Finally, my child, besides Baptism and the Holy Scriptures, the sacrament and the book, you had Prayer; an inward thing, invisible, unspeakable, and yet real above all things besides; and pre-eminently the language of the soul to God, and of God to the soul, the direct and personal communion of the humblest Christian with his Father in heaven.

What was it, then, that you lacked? I remember what you once said to me, when you were still a Protestant: "You, a monk, and I, a Puritan, are yet of the same blood royal!" You spoke truly. Not because you were a Puritan, but because, although a Puritan, you were a Christian, were we two of the same divine and royal stock. You were, like me, a child of the family, but, one stormy night, imprudent hands had carried your cradle far away from your Father's home: that home, although its form had faded from your vision, and your lips had forgotten how to speak its name, you have nevertheless been yearning after with tears and cries, and with every impulse of your soul. What you needed, my daughter, was to find it again, to weep upon

---

* 2 Corinthians, xi. 2.   † 1 John, ii. 20.

its threshold, to embrace its ancient walls, and dwell therein forever.

You found it, at last, in that temple of Saint Peter, the most vast and splendid ever reared by man to his God, but whose noblest grandeur, after all, to believing eyes, is this, that it images the universal brotherhood of the children of God upon the earth, " that he should gather together in one the children of God that were scattered abroad."* Coming from that great dispersion of souls, which is the work of man in Protestantism, you could contemplate their highest unity, which is the work of God in Catholicism. Suddenly thrilled to the depth of your soul, you looked around (I do but repeat your own touching story)—you looked around you for a priest of your own tongue, not to confess to—for you did not then know the need of that—but to tell your joy in having at last found a dwelling-place of the soul, that *home* so dear to your race, and more necessary in the religious than in the domestic life: "This is my rest forever: here will I dwell; for I have desired it."†

II. I have attempted to recount your past, and to show how God's loving-kindness has been preparing you, by his far-reaching hand, for the wonders of the present. What is this wondrous thing? It is your mystical marriage with Jesus Christ, by communion with his real body and blood in the sacrament of his true Church. Betrothed to God in baptism, you become his spouse in the Eucharist. "Blessed are they which are called unto the marriage supper of the Lamb."‡

It is not without a tender significance that you have chosen this 14th of July to consummate this solemn act. This day is the anniversary of your marriage—that mar-

---

* John, xi. 52.   † Psalm cxxxii. 14.   ‡ Revelation, xix. 9.

riage which has been sundered by death. Still young, and the mother of a fatherless child, you might have contracted new ties that would have given a father to your little one, and to yourself a husband. You have decided otherwise. You have made your entrance into the Catholic Church the epoch of a great transformation in your spiritual life, and have desired, on this day so full of loving and sorrowful memories, to lay your suffering hand in the hand of the crucified Spouse, never again to be withdrawn.

How beautiful appears that Spouse of Calvary, in his blood and through your tears, and how truly is he made for you, my daughter! It is not only "Patience smiling at grief,"* it is Love transported with sorrow and reposing in death. I remember the day when first I saw you in the parlor of my humble convent: you wore already on your bosom a Catholic crucifix, and your eyes, full of light and tears, glanced from time to time toward that other cross on the wall which looked down upon our meeting, with an expression that revealed your whole soul—all it still lacked—all it already foresaw.

I do not wish to overstate anything; above all, I would give no offence to any man. But may I not say that the orbit wherein Protestant piety ordinarily moves is the divine, rather than God himself? It is conscience with its steely temper, at once evangelical and personal; it is reverence for truth, the instinctive love for moral and religious things. I call all this the divine, not God; it is the glorious rays of the sun, not its dazzling disk. Where is the upspringing of the soul to the living God? "My soul thirsteth for God, for the living God: when shall I come and appear before God?"† Where is

---

* Shakspeare.   † Psalm xlii. 2.

the habitual communion of the heart and life with the Word made flesh?—the tears shed, like the Magdalene's, upon his feet?—the head bowed, like John's, upon his breast?—all that which the "*Imitation of Jesus Christ*" calls so well "the familiar friendship of Jesus?" Where, to express it in a single word, is that Real Presence which flows from the sacrament as from a hidden spring, like a river of peace, upon the true Catholic, all the day long, gladdening and fertilizing all his life?

This Immanuel—God with us—awaited you in our church, and in that sacrament which so powerfully attracted you, even when you but half believed it. In your own worship, as in the ancient synagogue, you found naught but types and shadows; they spoke to you of reality, but did not contain it; they awakened your thirst, but did not quench it: weak and empty rudiments, which have no longer the right to exist, since the veil of the temple has been rent asunder, and eternal realities been revealed. "Old things are passed away; behold, all things are become new."* Ah! blessed art thou, to have been led to the nuptial chamber of the Lamb!

And yet, my daughter, if Christ has enticed your heart (it is the prophet's own word, "O Lord, thou enticed me and I was enticed; thou art stronger than I, and hast prevailed"†), he has respected all the rights of your reason and free will. You have weighed long in the balance of your judgment what you have resolved, what you are about to accomplish. I must do you the justice to say that you have been scrupulous in reflection, and maturely deliberate in the fulfilment of your

---

* 2 Corinthians, v. 17.

† Jeremiah, xx. 7. The expression of the common English version is hardly justified by the Hebrew text.—Tr.

design:—so much have you feared lest this great religious act should bear any other character than personal conviction; so strongly have you persisted in avoiding any shadow of human influence from without, or any shadow of the influence of imagination or sentiment within!

It is thus that Jesus Christ has sought you for himself. Spouse of love, he is, at the same time, the Spouse of truth and of freedom; and this is why, when he draws souls to himself, he never beguiles nor compels them. He is the eternal Word, begotten of the reason of the Father, born in the outflow of his infinite splendor; he remembers his origin, and when he comes to us, it is not under cover of our darkness, but in the sincerity of his light. And because he is Truth, he is Liberty: he bows with respect* before the liberty of the soul, his image and offspring, and unlearns the language of command to employ none but that of prayer. "Open to me, my sister, my love, my dove, my undefiled," he says in the sacred Song; "for my head is filled with dew, and my locks with the drops of the night."† "Behold," he says in the Revelation, "I stand at the door and knock; if any man hear my voice, and open the door, I will come in to him, and will sup with him, and he with me."‡ He does not force an entrance into the heart, but he enters if it is opened to him. O rapturous words, which show that with God love has the same delicacy as with man! True love respects as well as loves, and will accept its triumph only at the hands of our free choice.

But is this all? Liberty is not sufficient to this jealous love: there must be struggle and sacrifice. What

---

* Wisdom, xii. 18.   † Solomon's Song, v. 2.   ‡ Revelation, iii. 20.

were the cruel conflicts which rendered your choice, though free, so difficult and painful? I may not answer this. Family, friends, country,—I have seen these sacred wounds too near to dare to touch them. I will only say that I never knew, till now, how much it costs the most completely settled mind, and the will most firmly resolved, to leave the religion of mother and of native land!

Ah! why, on the noble soil of the United States, must our church be still—I do not say unknown—but despised by so many souls? Would to God that it were simply unknown! A new apostle might then go to invoke upon those shores that "unknown God" whom Paul invoked before the Areopagus, that Church which they love in the ideal without knowing it in the reality; and, free from prejudices, thoughtful America would receive it better than frivolous Athens. But they think they know us, and they see us through such a cloud of evil report, that our name excites nothing but disgust and hatred. How long shall these age-long misunderstandings endure? and when shall God at last command the division-wall to be thrown down? It certainly depends upon ourselves to prepare for that longed-for day by drawing nearer to each other;—not, certainly, by making doctrinal concessions, which would be sinful if they were not chimerical, but by the abandonment of our mutual prejudices in the presence of facts better understood, and by the formation of those kindly relations in which esteem and charity might even now unite those whom difference of belief still separates. As for myself, this is my most ardent wish; and the more I come to appreciate the condition of religious affairs in this country, the more living and urgent necessity this question assumes. Since, then, "the time is come that judgment must begin at the house of God,"* let us, Roman Catholics, learn how to give the example: let us boldly arise and reach out a loyal hand to our separated but well-beloved brethren.

But what am I saying? have not you, yourself, Madam, in coming to us, first surmounted obstacles which I could not recount? You have overcome them by the sweat of your brow and the blood of your soul; for, as Saint Augustine so truly says, "there is a blood of the soul," and this you have poured out. You have pushed aside with your heroic hands, like the daughter of Zion, the hewn rocks with which you were enclosed,† you have made straight your paths, and have come hither.

Let me welcome you with your own words, in which you expressed but a few days since the inspiration which was your strength: "My love, my beautiful one, calls me: I know his voice, and weak and trembling as I am, I come to Him."

III. Let us end our song of the mercies of the Lord to your soul. Betrothed by baptism even in the midst of your involuntary errors, espoused by the Eucharist in the integrity of Catholic faith and charity, how can you complete the cycle of supernatural love and consummate your life therein, except by becoming a mother in the apostleship?

The Lord was speaking to the multitude one day, when he was told his mother and brethren were without, desiring to speak with him. Glancing about him with that inspired look of his, he exclaimed: "Who is my mother, and who are my brethren?" Then stretching his hand over the trembling multitude, he said, "Behold my mother and my brethren! For whosoever shall do

---

* 1 Peter, iv. 17.   † Lamentations, iii. 9.

the will of my Father which is in heaven, the same is my brother, and sister, and mother."* Saint Gregory the Great, explaining this teaching of the Master in one of his homilies,† found some difficulty in this word, "my mother." We are without doubt his brethren and sisters, in that we fulfil his Father's will; but how can any being other than Mary be called his "mother?" But the great pope remarks immediately, that whenever one soul, by word or example or any spiritual influence whatsoever, produces and develops in another soul the Word of God, the actual and living Truth and Righteousness and Love, in one word, Jesus Christ (for Jesus Christ is all these), it becomes, with a higher reality than that of maternal conception, the mother of Jesus in that soul, and the mother of that soul in Jesus.

And now, Madam, God, if I mistake not, reserves for you some chosen part in this gift of spiritual motherhood. There are beloved ones of whom I may not speak, —respect and emotion forbid me; but you shall be their mother in Jesus, their mother in the integrity of their liberty, as you were his spouse in the fulness of your own. Then there are other souls, numberless and without name, at least to our feeble thought, who are counted and inscribed in the book of the divine election, and whom the mysterious power of your apostleship will gather from the four winds of heaven. For not in vain the Lord has spoken: "Many shall come from the East and from the West, and shall sit down with Abraham, and Isaac, and Jacob, in the kingdom of heaven; but the children of the kingdom shall be cast out into outer darkness." ‡ Yes, many born, like you, in heresy without having been heretics, ignorant without having been guilty, shall hasten to the feast of Catholic truth, to the

* Matthew. xii. 49. 50.   † Hemil. iii. in Evang.   ‡ Matthew, viii. 11, 12.

joys of recovered unity; while, alas! many of us who, zealous for the letter, have used it to stifle the spirit, shall peradventure find themselves shut out from the kingdom of God, the fruits whereof they did not bring forth.*

Go then, as a missionary of peace and light, to the land which awaits you, the country whose moral future, by an especial design of Providence, is almost entirely in the hands of its women. You will have no occasion to regret the absence of that opportunity of public preaching from which your sex excludes you. You will speak in the modest and persuasive eloquence of conversation, you will speak by your person and your noble life, at once free and submissive, humble and yet proud, austere and tolerant, carrying the love of God to the highest aspirations, and the love of your neighbor to the gentlest condescension.

But I wish to define more particularly the special character of your apostleship. Telling me the story of your soul, with its hates and loves, you said, "I have hated three things—slavery, the Catholic Church, and immorality." Of these three hates but one remains. Slavery no longer exists; God has effaced this mark of Cain from the brow of your people with the baptism of blood. And when you came to know the Catholic Church, you changed your hatred into love. You have espoused her in order to struggle more effectively with her against this last enemy. Now, in the firm foundation of its dogmas replacing the quicksand whereon your uncertain feet have been treading, in the richness of its sacraments substituted for the barrenness of your worship, under the direction of its hierarchy, and in the strength of its unity, you will combat the double

* Matthew, xxi. 43.

immorality which dishonors us: that immorality of the mind which is called rationalism in Europe, and in America, infidelity—two diseases, unlike, it is true, but equally mortal; and that immorality of the heart which corrupts the senses as the former corrupts the thought! These two immoralities are sisters; one assaults the chastity of the faith, the other, the chastity of love; and both have found in woman an especial enemy. To the serpent which crawls on its belly and eats the dust, the Lord has said from the beginning, in pointing to woman, that ideal being sprung from the heart of man, "I will put enmity between thee and the woman, and between thy seed and her seed; she shall bruise thy head, and thou shalt bruise his heel."*

Now behold that woman blessed among women! Mary, the young wife, Mary the young mother, passing through the hill-country of Judea, to visit her kinswoman stricken in years, and hopeless as it seemed in sterility. She carries in her womb the infinite burden of the Word, but her step is light as truth and love. In an ecstasy of holy transport, she greets Elizabeth, who feels, at her approach, the germ of life quicken within her. "And whence is this to me, that the mother of my Lord should come to me?" The children were yet mute, but their mothers prophesy—Elizabeth before John the Baptist, Mary before Jesus Christ. "Already," to use the language of St. Ambrose, "already some faint movements toward man's salvation begin to make themselves felt,"† and because sin had commenced by woman, by woman, also, regeneration is to begin.

And now I seem to see the Christian woman, espoused of Jesus and his mother, drawing near to this

---

* Genesis, iii. 15. The Vulgate here varies from the original.—Tr.
† "Serpunt enim jam tentamenta salutis humanæ." In Luc.

generation, that has grown old like Elizabeth in sorrow and barrenness. The obstacles which have baffled us will be no hindrance before her. In the inspirations of her love, she will drink in a faith and hope which too often have been wanting to us. Rising, like Mary, to the heights of peace, walking in the footsteps of the dawn and of the spring-tide, she will sound in the ears of the men of this century that language of the heart in which we recognize the presence of the Lord. "For lo, as soon as the voice of thy salutation sounded in mine ears, the babe leaped in my womb for joy."*

"Rise, O captive daughter of Zion, loose thyself from the bands of thy neck! How beautiful upon the mountains are the feet of her that publisheth peace, that bringeth glad tidings of salvation, that saith, The Lord shall reign!"†

* Luke, i. 44. † Isaiah, lii. 2, 7

SERMON

IN BEHALF OF THE VICTIMS OF THE SOUTH AMERICAN EARTHQUAKE,

Preached at the Church of La Madeleine, Paris, March 11, 1869.

"O Lord, I have heard thy voice, and was afraid; . . . in wrath remember mercy."—HABAKKUK, iii. 2.

BRETHREN: This voice of God in his judgments has burst upon our ears with unwonted force. And yet it would seem that, after a lapse of seven months, the sound should have begun to die away. At an epoch when events are crowding one upon another, swift and multiform as never before, in a city as marvellous as the age itself, in which all the echoes of the world come to resound, as in a universal centre, am I not quite behind time in speaking of the South American disasters? On the contrary, this is the very time to speak. It is not till now that those people are fairly waking up from the first shock of their calamity, reckoning up their losses, one by one, and looking about them for the means of relief. And for ourselves, too, this is the time for sober meditation and for Christian thought. For at the first tidings of the disaster, under the influence of those generous feelings that belong to human nature—may I not say, especially to the nature of Frenchmen?—we, too, were stunned by the announcement.

Let us pause, brethren, in the presence of death and

in the presence of God, in the presence of his transient severity and his everlasting loving-kindness; and that we may the better be prepared to shed our tears over so many graves, our balm over so many wounds, let us fortify ourselves, both in reason and in heart, with holy thoughts of the Christian faith. Others have busied themselves—and rightly, for it was their special mission—in seeking the reason of the calamity in the combination of physical causes. It is for us, without ignoring the laws of nature, to go deeper, even to the laws of God. "I will enter into the strength of the Lord God: I will remember nothing, save thy righteousness."* But the righteousness of God is big with mercy, like those threatening clouds which carry beneath their thunderbolts the treasures of the rain and the fruitfulness of all the land.†

"I have heard thy voice, and was afraid. In wrath remember mercy."

Righteousness in the chastisement of sin, mercy in the trial of virtue, these are the true aspects under which I would consider with you the earthquake which in the month of August, 1868, desolated two great countries of South America, Ecuador and Peru.

I. The chastisement of sin.

Chastisement, sin, justice! What have these words to do in presence of a grief which they insult, but cannot explain? Is it worth while for the priest to go back to the superstition of former ages, now condemned beyond appeal by the reason of the scholar and the conscience

---

* Psalm lxxi. 16. See the Vulgate version.
† See a familiar hymn of Cowper:

> "The clouds ye so much dread
> Are big with mercy, and shall break
> In blessings on your head."—Tr.

of the honest man? No, cries modern science; the world is not the plaything of capricious wills! Everything, on the contrary, bears the majestic impress of the universality and immutability of law. It is not, then, to God, but to nature, that we must go for the reason of these physical catastrophes, once called judgments of God. Let us penetrate deeper into the causes of them! Some day, perhaps, we shall be able to control their effects!

Science is right, brethren; the world does not belong to miracle, but to law. Only let us leave law in possession of its own exalted seat! Let us not confound it, like Epicurus, with the combinations of a lucky chance, nor, like Zeno, with the exigences of a blind necessity. Be it what it is, that supreme thought which creates order because it has first conceived it—which respects itself in respecting its work, and which limits its infinite power only by its infinite wisdom and infinite goodness! Then, in every sphere of existence, the material as well as the spiritual, the grand definition of the reign of God will be, that it is the reign of laws!

But these laws, it will perhaps be said, so far as they refer to the subject which now engages our attention, are natural laws, not moral laws. Admitting that they stand related to God the Creator in their origin, nevertheless they do not cease to be, in his intentions as well as their own nature, related to the exercise of his justice and the chastisement of sin.

How long, forsooth, has the kingdom of God been divided on this question against itself? How long has duality been the highest expression of supreme oneness? Doubtless suffering and death, in the inferior races, are older than the sin of Adam, and stand in no direct connection with the moral system. Without doubt, the convulsions of nature have preceded the existence of man: we find their marks on the crust of the earth, so often fitted up for the residence of life, and, in turn, so often torn to ruins. They constitute that Genesis of science, in appearance so contrary, in reality so conformed to the Genesis of the Bible. But when Adam appeared, born at once of the ruddy clay and of the breath of God, the earth kept silence before him: the sacred tie that binds together the physical and moral laws was drawn fast in his consciousness. Therein, perfect innocence and perfect happiness had stricken covenant, and amid the peace of Eden was heard only the song of nature at rest with man and God in a sabbath which bade fair to be eternal. This sabbath-day—how came it to an end? How came nature to be in revolt against its King? How was death with its attendant plagues able to intrude into this upper world from which it had been warned away? "By one man sin entered into the world, and death by sin."* You have heard the stern language of Saint Paul, you have recognized the cardinal doctrine of original sin. It is, then, simply a matter of logical consistency—it is simply following out the Bible to its conclusions—when, notwithstanding those laws of science which are mistakenly offered in evidence against us, we persist in seeing, in the evils which rest in common upon all our race, in the disasters which smite individuals or isolated countries, the various applications of one constant law of the moral system—that death is the punishment of sin.

But what! If it is possible for science to tolerate these strange doctrines, under pretence that they are out of its province, is it possible for conscience to sub-

* Romans, v. 12.

scribe to them? Does it not revolt and lift up its indignant protest? Had Ecuador and Peru a larger share in the sin of Adam, that they were mulcted in so vast a forfeit? Had they filled up the measure of their debt by more multitudinous transgressions and more crying sins? And in these mourning countries, must I point out to you, in each of these twenty thousand sufferers, instead of the unfortunate victim of an accident, a criminal marked for vengeance?

May God deliver me from such excess of fanaticism and cruelty!

"Think ye," said our divine Master, "that those eighteen on whom the tower in Siloam fell and slew them, were sinners above all men that dwelt in Jerusalem? I tell ye, Nay; but, except ye repent, ye shall all likewise perish."* Guilt is universal: so, also, will punishment be, at least in the future life, unless penitence should avert it before the hour of justice comes. But the thunderbolts which, in this life, from time to time break through the sheltering clouds of loving-kindness, do not always smite the guiltiest, do not necessarily spare the most innocent. Why, then, do they smite at all, since they do but obey His voice who sendeth forth the lightnings that they may go upon his errands, and, returning, answer, Here we are?† Why? I don't know, brethren; I don't know: and nobody else knows any better than I do.

An inscrutable Providence presides over the distribution of the judgments of God in the regions of space and time. "His judgments," says the psalm, "are a great deep;"‡ and it was on the verge of this deep that one gazed down from the third heaven, and, as if with swimming brain, cried out, "*O the depth!*"§

* Luke, xiii. 4, 5.   † Job, xxxviii. 35.   ‡ Psalm xxxvi. 6.   § Romans, xi. 33.

We talk of a sin, and of sins. The word of God answers back to us and speaks of *the* sin, the one sin, the sin of the world. "Behold the Lamb of God, that taketh away the sin of the world!"* Our faults are not separable and independent; there is not one of them but has somewhat to do—is, somehow, mysteriously implicated—with the transgressions of the race; just as, in its turn, the collective weight of human guilt lies on each several conscience, and oppresses and burdens it from the cradle upwards. Doubtless conscience is an individual matter. It bears its own personal responsibility. As the prophet says, "The righteousness of the righteous shall be upon him, and the wickedness of the wicked shall be upon him."† But face to face with this individual conscience, there appears a universal—if I may use the word—a humanitarian conscience. Over against the responsibility proper to each, is set the responsibility common to all. Our moral nature is full of these antinomies which distract it without destroying it, because they are harmonized in a higher unity. It responds at once to the God of Ezekiel, who declares that the son shall not bear the iniquity of the father, nor the father the iniquity of the son;‡ and to the God of Moses, who glories in visiting the sins of the fathers upon their children to the third and fourth generation.§

Solidarity—the universal community of interests! It is the great law which positive science establishes everywhere in nature,—which a generous statesmanship demands everywhere in society. Why might it not be, under forms more mysterious, but not less real, the law of the moral and religious world?

In this way, without having recourse to any narrow or obsolete ideas, we explain the great Bible doctrine of

---

* John, i. 29.   † Ezekiel, xviii. 20.   ‡ Ibid.   § Numbers, xiv. 18.

the unity of mankind in the apostasy and in the atonement. There is something more than the man, there is humanity;—humanity, which falls as one in Adam, and in every one of the sons of Adam; humanity that is lifted up as one in Jesus Christ, and in every one of the brethren of Jesus Christ. Wheresoever falls the stroke of supreme justice, what individual or what country soever it may smite, it punishes and redeems, at once, the whole race of man in each one of its victims—each a victim of wrath, marked beforehand for punishment, if he be more guilty; each a victim of propitiation, offering himself for expiation, if he be more innocent, or rather, if he be less impure.

May I venture—not to sound unfathomable righteousness, but to lean trembling over the brink of that abyss? May I venture vaguely to inquire, so far as it is possible to the timid and uncertain thought of mortal man,* what is the special crime that could deserve the punishment of which I am this day speaking?

I would not give offence to any, whether God or man; but something urges me on. I am a European, as their fathers were, of Latin race and Catholic religion. I feel myself constrained to confess their crime as if it were my own.

There was of old, in that land, a strange empire that seemed still to retain something of the splendors of the king of day, from which it conceived itself to have sprung. Absolute as the sun himself in power, and exercising it only for the happiness of their subjects, the Children of the Sun presented the rare spectacle of a beneficent despotism. Rare spectacle, indeed, and I thank God for it,

---

* "For what man could know the counsel of God? Or who could think what is the will of God? For the thoughts of mortals are timid, and our foresight is uncertain." *Book of Wisdom,* ix. 13, 14.

for it would be sad enough if history were to justify the fatal and cowardly instinct which drags nations into the arms of despotism! However that may be, the Incas had breathed into their government the spirit of religion under the noblest and sweetest form that the worship of nature could possibly assume. They looked upon that orb of which the Psalmist has sung as the tabernacle Jehovah,* and not daring to raise their homage to the invisible God, whom they nevertheless acknowledged,† they hailed with joyful adoration the dazzling symbol of his power and goodness—the Sun! Under the influence of this paternal absolutism and these ennobling superstitions, a civilization was moulded, far inferior to ours, I need not say, but far superior to that of the other countries of America, especially of the Mexican empire. It was a stock all ready to be grafted with the divine scion of Christianity.

At this very time—for all things are woven into the designs of Providence and the woof of humanity—Europe was ready for a work hitherto unknown. God had been preparing her for it for fifteen centuries. From the beginning, he had sent forth to her from Zion his Bible and his Church, by the hand of his greatest apostles; he had renewed the youth of her races by the blood of the Barbarians, of her languages by the theology of the Greek and Latin fathers; he had fashioned her institutions under the discipline, sometimes mild, sometimes harsh, of the Roman pontiffs. As the hour drew near, he showered lavishly upon her the discoveries of genius—the compass to guide her across the seas, printing to multiply and immortalize her thought, the

---

* Psalm xix. 4.

† The Peruvians, like so many other of the Indian races, recognized a Supreme Being, Creator and Ruler of the Universe. . . . . They reared no temple to this invisible Being.—*Prescott, History of the Conquest of Peru.*

cannon to overcome the resistance of matter and barbarism. And at last, setting at her head Christopher Columbus, that inspired captain, as if to found there a new mankind, he brought her to a new world.

The two worlds had met. The two mankinds were coming near each other—that which awaited, and that which brought Jesus Christ.

But, great God! what do I behold? After premeditated massacres to which the history of crime affords no parallel, I behold .... but I cannot speak of it. Pools of blood through which are crawling unarmed and defenceless men; depths of mire in which women—mothers and maids alike—are groaning; deep mines down which slaves descend, far from the light of that sun which they love, farther still from that Christ which they have been driven to hate! And above all these horrors of carnage, debauchery, cupidity—O abomination of desolation standing in the holy place!—the cross of Jesus Christ serving them as a pretext, and covering them with its shadow!

* * * * *

It is said that during the recent horrible catastrophe which has fallen upon these countries, in the burying-ground of one of those ruined cities,* men saw the mummied corpses of the Indians torn from their graves by the shocks of earthquake and the wash of the sea. It seemed as if they had risen up with a sort of ghastly joy to witness the just, though tardy vengeance that had come upon the children of their oppressors!

* * * * *

Enough, brethren, enough. Let us speak no more of vengeance! If there be vengeance here, it is God's vengeance, and we can but adore in silence. "The wrath of man worketh not the righteousness of God."†

* The city of Iquique. † James, i. 20.

Let us heap no more reproach on the great soul of the Spanish people, nor forget that this was not the only guilty race—that almost everywhere the white men, unworthy of their great trust, were oppressors, not liberators. The other great colonizing race of the American continent—the Anglo-Saxon—was this more humane and equitable at the North than the Spanish race at the South? Has it not crowded off the Indians into the wilderness? Has it not, with slow, inexorable perseverance, prosecuted the work of their entire extinction?

Just at this moment a message reaches us by the transatlantic cable. It is the language of that man who was the sword in the work in which Abraham Lincoln was the will, and who seems impatient to discharge his country's debt toward all men—red as well as black. His language is brief and unimpassioned as the coolest common sense—inflexible as conscience and honor:

"The proper treatment of the original occupants of this land, the Indians, is one deserving of careful study. I will favor any course toward them which tends to their civilization, Christianization, and ultimate citizenship."

And he adds these words, which are a most just statement of the policy of the Gospel, and, I venture to hope, of the policy of the future:

"In regard to foreign policy, I would deal with nations as equitable law requires individuals to deal with each other."*

Such language as this, Ecuador has no need to use. Long since, it carried it into its practice. Nobly unfaithful to the traditions of Pizarro and the early con-

---

* President Grant's Inaugural, March 4, 1869.

querors, it has repudiated slavery; daily, the sweat of the European meets and mingles with that of the Indian in the same furrow; often, there are even formed between the two races those conjugal alliances which elevate one without depressing the other, and which prepare the way for the great unity of the future. But if words be needed, in the presence of such facts, there are those of the Liberator, *el Libertador*, as they call the illustrious Bolivar: " Popular education should be the earliest care of a Congress. The two poles of a republic" [what *I* would say is—the two poles of any free country] "are morality and light. Morality and light are our prime necessities."*

Let these noble words, and the acts which followed them, wipe out forever the recollections which I have been compelled to recall! Rise, O future age, more glorious even than the present! Be lifted up, thou cross of Christ, so many a time profaned, over the manses of a chaste and devoted clergy, over convents of poor and laborious recluses, over schools taught by pious and learned masters; and shedding wide thy blessings over these reconciled populations, stand, the monument of a harder and a holier work than the punishment of crime —its reparation!

II. *The Trial of Virtue.* God's judgments, brethren, are not only,—not even chiefly—punishments; in a far higher sense they are trials. It is not well for man too long to droop the head before them; let him rather rise up, at once with humility and with pride, to resume his toil, and recommence his conflict. Man is both workman and soldier; workman in a mighty toil, soldier in

---

* " La educacion popular debe ser el cuidado primogenito de un congresso. Moral y luces son los polos de una republica; moral y luces son nuestras primeras necessidades."—*The Words of the Liberator to the Congress of Angostura.*

a mighty conflict. It is not in a chance way, for an easy-going, objectless existence, that he is placed in the world. For us Christians, at least, men of a serious, practical, spiritual philosophy, there is such a thing as final causes. We believe in them with a profound faith, and even a holy pride. We cannot be so cheaply satisfied as other men. We need and must have a great object, worthy of ourselves and God. But what shall it be? On an earth once trodden by the feet of Christ, amid the course of ages that are illuminated from his cross, is there for the soul of man and for all the race, any other object than God's salvation? "Ye receive," says the apostle Peter, "the end of your faith, the salvation of your souls."*

Salvation of souls! But how? For the vast majority—almost the entire mass of men, salvation is not achieved in the deserts and in ecstatic visions, but in the midst of society. It is realized by faithfulness to the duties of family and civil life, to all those holy obligations which bind us to our fellow-men; by the practical effort of a life which turns heavenward in prayer for light and strength, and then turns back to earth in labor for wealth, and liberty, and above all for righteousness. "For God," says the inspired book, "has formed man, in his wisdom to have dominion over the creation which he had made, and order the earth in equity and righteousness." † Understood in this sense, cleared of that narrow and exclusive conception which has been fastened on it by a false mysticism, so far is the salvation of the individual from being isolated from the salvation of the race, that it is well-nigh confounded with it. The temporal conquest of the earth, in that noble sense which I have just explained, is found to be the condition of the

---

* Peter, i. 9. † Wisdom, ix. 2, 3.

eternal conquest of heaven,—or rather, earth and heaven do but form one kingdom of God. It is the apocalyptic city, descending from heaven and resting on the earth and reconciling into one the interests of this life and of the life to come, which becomes the centre of universal history, the common dwelling-place of God and men. "I, John, saw the holy city, new Jerusalem, descending out of heaven from God, like a bride adorned for her husband. And I heard a great voice out of heaven saying, Behold the tabernacle of God is with men, and he will dwell with them, and they shall be his people, and he shall be with them and be their God!"*

This royal city descends from heaven; and yet each day the hand of man is building it upon the earth. The effort which it requires is so laborious, and so bitterly opposed, that there is need at once of workmen and of soldiers. As in those troubled days when Nehemiah, despite the hostility of the surrounding tribes, rebuilt the walls of the old Jerusalem, so we must wear at once the cuirass and the workman's apron, and handle the trowel with which to build the wall, while we bear the sword with which to repel the enemy.†

We are beset by a triple foe. A threefold barbarism is making incessant attacks on that work of civilization —both man's and God's—which is prosecuted in time, to be completed in eternity:—the barbarism of infernal spirits, the barbarism of men of error and mischief, the barbarism of nature in revolt against its Lord.

Of infernal spirits I have no occasion to speak;—not that I fear the sneers of incredulity, but because this matter does not relate to my subject. We know well enough, from another teacher, that our wrestling is "not against flesh and blood"—against visible man;

* Revelation, xxi. 2, 3. † Nehemiah, iv. 16, 17.

but against that higher power of sin and error which dwells in the moral atmosphere we breathe, in the heaven of our loftiest thoughts, our purest affections— "against spiritual wickedness in heavenly places,"* which there transforms itself into an "angel of light."† Neither have I aught to say concerning that barbarism of the unbelieving nations which surrounds the civilization of Europe as with a dense atmosphere into which its light has not yet been able to penetrate; nor of that other barbarism which our society bears within it, in its morals, its sciences, its institutions, and which realizes the ancient maxim, "*Optimi cujusque pessima corruptio*"—the worst of all corruptions is the corruption of the most perfect organization.

But this planet itself, on which the work of our great race is wrought, would almost seem less to have been made for us than to have been made against us. From its strange infancy, an incandescent mass or an abyss of liquid fire, a huge firebrand hurtling through space or dashing out its confused waves into the darkness, it has seemed the enemy of life in every form. Then during those six days—God's days, not man's, and therefore not to be measured—for "a thousand years in his sight are but as yesterday"‡—it has, with convulsive pangs of labor, produced, and again destroyed, huge forms of being, plants or animals, which never could have subsisted in the same atmosphere with ourselves. Finally, after all these cataclysms, when that strip of earth habitable for man had emerged—I say nothing of the vast deserts which dispute our occupancy of it, nor of the frozen regions which consume it at the poles, nor of the heats that blaze along its tropical shores— I find it so scanty in its length, in its breadth—I was

* Ephesians, vi. 12.   † 2 Corinthians, xi. 14.   ‡ Psalm xc. 4.

about to say, so scanty in its accommodations—that it seems to me less like a peaceful and permanent dwelling, than a frail ship beaten by the storms of three oceans —the sea of waters round about, the sea of air above, the sea of fire underneath! Once already it has foundered in the waves; may it not, peradventure, be sometime swallowed up in the flames? For "the day of the Lord shall come as a thief in the night, in the which the heavens shall pass away with a great noise, and the elements shall melt with fervent heat; the earth also, and the works that are therein, shall be burned up."*

Was this calamity the presage of that day? And must I needs repeat the fearful story of it in your ears? See those happy populations, on the evening of one of their most cherished festivals, the Assumption of the Virgin, their well-beloved patron-saint. While for the Mother of Christ the shadows of death are shot through with beams of happiness and radiant life, for them life itself is on the point of changing suddenly to death. Their beds are made their tombs; their cities, in a moment, are transformed to ruins. Convulsed with internal fires, the earth reels like a drunkard in his cups; the sea rears itself in sudden rage, and leaps upon the shore, flinging the ships in wild wreck among the crumbling houses.

See them now, these decimated families, camping out in tents, hiding in caves, houseless and homeless, and without the implements of labor! Look upon it, that nation in mourning, its cities overthrown, its harbors choked with sand, its roads obstructed, its country ravaged, plunged in misery! This I call their trial—a trial rather than a punishment; an occasion for religious resignation, but at the same time of manly energy; a

---

* 2 Peter, iii. 10.

life-and-death struggle with the powers of nature, in which man, overcome at first, and always the weaker party, triumphs at last, by force of intelligence and bravery and virtue!

It is our trial, too, brethren—the trial of our charity. I have spoken of the solidarity of mankind in sin and in punishment. I have done so with hesitation, almost with violence to my own feelings, so that I might come at this nobler solidarity of the world in love. The love that is in Christ Jesus binds together not individuals alone, but nations. It cannot rest save in the grand unity of the human family. Ah! how fain was I, also, to rest, before my task was done, at that vital point where meet, at last, after so many a conflict, the spirit of my church and the spirit of my age! Need was for me to set forth in my words, what you are about to set forth in action, the doctrine taught nigh two thousand years ago by the apostle to the Gentiles, which now, at last, is just beginning to come to the comprehension of mankind. "By revelation," says he, "there has been made known to me a mystery which in other ages was not made known to the children of men." What is this mystery which Saint Paul calls "the mystery of Christ?" "That the nations should be fellow-heirs and *concorporeal*"—O sublime barbarism of speech!—"of one body, one humanity, sharers together in the promises of God in Christ Jesus by the Gospel."* Henceforth, then, there is no longer stranger nor foreigner in mankind such as the Gospel conceives it, such as some day the Gospel will make it. Henceforth there shall be no more sea, nor intervening mountains, to keep asunder the nations, but mutual love and mutual helpfulness in the advancement of their common work.

* Ephesians, iii. 3–6.

Nevertheless, let me add, since I am speaking as a Frenchman to Frenchmen, that the populations of Ecuador and Peru have more special claims on our sympathy and assistance. Like us, they are both by blood and by language of the Latin stock. Like us, they belong to the Catholic church. Amid the mingling of races, their blood, like ours, has been kept with a purer pedigree. Our languages grow together out of the illustrious stock of ancient Rome, and are derived through that from the speech of Homer and Plato, the finest, perhaps, the most philosophical and melodious, that ever ennobled human lips. They have abode with us in the old religious edifice, in that Catholic church which guards amid its ruins, with the grandest traditions of the past, the grandest hopes of the future. Ah, well I know—and many a time have I groaned within myself to think of it—these nations of the Latin race and of the Catholic religion have been of late the most grievously tried of all! Not only by intestine fires, by the quaking of the earth, by the inrushing of the sea. Look with impartial eye, with the fearless serenity of truth, with that assurance of faith which fears not to accept the revelations of experience, and then tell me—where is it that the moral foundations quake most violently? Where does the current of a formidable electricity give the severest, the most incessant shocks to republics as well as monarchies? Among the Latin races; among the Catholic nations. Yes, by some inscrutable design of Providence, they, more than others, have had to "drink of the cup deep and large;"* they have wet their lips more deeply in the chalice in which are mingled "the wine, the lightning, and the spirit of the storm;" and they have become possessed with the madness of the

---

* Ezekiel, xxiii. 32.

drunkard. It is not a decadence, as some have said; it is a crisis, and the violence of it bears witness, not only to the potency of the poison which consumes them, but to the strength of vitality which is to save them. If these races could perish, there would have been an end of them three centuries ago. Nay, the hour is at hand! "Awake! awake! Stand up, O Jerusalem, which hast drunk at the hand of the Lord the cup of his fury! thou hast drunken the dregs of the cup of trembling, and wrung them out!"* .... "when thou shalt have taken forth the precious from the vile, thou shalt be as the mouth of Jehovah himself."†

O Frenchmen, Catholics, let us come to the rescue of our Spanish-American brethren! In their material trials, let us help them with our gold; in their moral trials, with our heart and soul.

And you, to whatever blood and whatever faith you belong—all you who have come hither to this feast of charity, my friends, my brethren, forget the things that divide us, and think only of the things that unite us. As we join hands for the relief of this great calamity, let us labor to speed on the day of the Lord. O blessed day, when, in the vast and irresistible movement that is bringing men together and mingling them in every part of the world, all races shall flow together in one race, and all religions shall be transfigured, and shall embrace each other in that religion which is free from all error, rich in all truth—in Catholic Christianity. "There shall be one flock and one shepherd,"‡—one humanity in one Church, with one Christ, and under one God!

* Isaiah, li. 17.   † Jeremiah, xv. 19.   ‡ John, x. 9.

LETTER,

Prefixed to "The Select Works of Charles Loyson."

[Charles Loyson, uncle to Father Hyacinthe, was a pupil of the *Ecole Normale*, and was regarded by his schoolmates, Cousin and Jouffroy, and by his illustrious contemporaries, Guizot, Royer-Collard, Maine de Biran, and de Serre, as the most remarkable young man of the generation which came into public life about that very critical and hopeful era of French history, the year 1817. A man of wide versatility, and generous sympathies with the interests of human liberty and of the Christian faith, he was at once poet, orator, and statesman. His name shone for a brief time with rare brilliancy, and was then suddenly extinguished in death.

Fifty years afterward, a gentleman who was much interested in the history of the province of Brittany, the native province of the Loyson family, felt moved, in part by an honorable local pride, to rescue from oblivion the history of so bright though brief a career of one of his fellow-citizens, by compiling a volume of his works in prose and verse. The volume was prefaced with critical notices from the distinguished pens of MM. Patin and Sainte Beuve, and with the following Letter to the Editor by Father Hyacinthe.

In a brief review of this memorial volume, M. Augustin Cochin, known to multitudes of Americans by his constant and most intelligent vindication of our national cause before his own countrymen, remarks thus concerning the deceased poet:

"Let us not spend too much pity on the unknown orator, the forgotten author, the poet whose song was broken off by death, but whose memory now, let us hope, is about to be revived in the hearts of new readers. His life was not long, but it was lived at a great period. His writings are not many, but they are in behalf of noble interests. His friends were not numerous, but they are among the best and greatest men of his country. And after the lapse of fifty years, he has critics like Patin and Sainte Beuve to commemorate his genius, and an heir of his own name like Father Hyacinthe to eulogize his character and soul. We need not pity him!"]

To M. Emile Grimaud.

I assure you, Sir, that I have not forgotten that summer evening of which you remind me in such poetic language. I remember especially the amiable and generous enthusiasm with which you kindly consented to aid my brother and myself in a work which was both a family duty and a dream of our childhood. The provincial spirit, which is born and dies with the family spirit, and to the revival of which you have so nobly devoted your literary activity, had already endeared to you the memory of the scholar of Beaupréau, the son of Brittany and Vendée, afterward the friend and counsellor of the ministers and supporters of the Restoration in its best days. You have been willing to love his memory the better for our sake, and to devote yourself to making him known, which is, I do not fear to say, to make him beloved. I thank you for it, from the bottom of my heart.

It is not for me to decide whether this funeral monument, raised by our common care, shall have a permanent right to stand in the field of glory; but those of the younger generation, whose sympathetic and pious attention it will attract, will surely find in it examples and lessons worthy of their study. Glory is perhaps the best of human idols, but, after all, it is only an idol: our ambition should be to leave behind us the lesson of truth, the example of goodness.

The first lesson and example set before us in these pages, is that of an enlightened as well as ardent devotion to literature, and particularly in that which is the highest form of human thought and sentiment—poetry. The question has been often asked, in our day, whether the reason of the existence of this form of literature had not ceased in view of the severe and positive requirements of the spirit of the age;—whether the function of poetry was not about to terminate with that of religion, to which in many ways it is so near akin, and which it has served, more than once, as a most noble interpreter. This question, already agitated in his time, is discussed by Charles Loyson, and he concludes with the conviction that whatever there is in the heart of man that relates to the sense of the infinite, is permanent; while, at the same time, he points out with rare sagacity, the changes rendered indispensable in literature by the march of time. He is doubtless wrong when he banishes poetry from the realm of nature, which he mistakenly conceives to have been disenchanted by modern science and industry: he is right when he opens to it the inner world of the soul and the unexplored regions of our spiritual nature. He is wrong again when he condemns as a critic what he has excellently practised as a poet—the description of common life, the charm of domestic details, and the household muse from whose inspiration the great novelists of England and America, of late years, have derived results so rich in incident and so lofty in their moral tone; but he is grandly in the right when, rejecting with scorn the old mythological machinery, the object even at this time of superstitious respect, he demands in all things the substitution of truth for conventionality, and gives in these terms a sort of prelude to whatever is legitimate and necessary in the revolution accomplished by the romantic school. "The first poets," he wrote, "were philosophers; hereafter the philosophers are to be poets." This is almost identical with the definition which our Lamartine has given of the poetry of the future: "It will be *reason in song.*" If I were not afraid of perpetrating a pleonasm, I would add that it will be, especially, morality and religion in song, and I would name as the subjects of its immortal trilogy—subjects ever true and ever fresh—the temple, the home, the State.

If the poet can sing of the State, why not serve the State? Devotion to the muse, however, has been esteemed not quite compatible with the struggles in which political life involves us, and perhaps with the qualities it demands in us. It was reserved for our age to break down the walls which have too long separated the different lines of human thought and action. Of this, Charles Loyson was a forerunner; he could be at the same time publicist and poet, and I cannot venture to say in which of the two careers he was best fitted to excel. At any rate, he acquired at once, and in a high degree, the esteem and confidence of such men as M. de Serre, Royer-Collard, Guizot; and at twenty-nine years of age he already held rank and authority among the writers who adorned that stormy, but glorious and fruitful inauguration of the liberal monarchy of 1814. What especially impresses and charms me in him, is his horror of party spirit. In presence of the social antagonism which had survived our late misfortunes and was preparing new ones, that clear-seeing mind, that patriotic and generous heart, saw no hope of salvation except in *the great party of France,* as Father Gratry so well calls it; a party which—thank God!—has never needed to be created, but which then lacked, as it does to-day, a sufficient representation and influence in public life. Withal, I should not wish to identify myself absolutely with the policy which my uncle followed. He could not have guessed what misunderstandings and dangers would spring from the Charter of 1814. But accepting the political establishment of which that was the basis, he endeavored to maintain in their independence and in their harmony, on the one hand authority, the safeguard of liberty as well as of order, and liberty, which is, its very self, an inviolable and sacred authority. For this reason, without scrupling for his youth, without hesitating before the talent and renown of his powerful adversaries, he attacks at the same time, and not without success, absolutism in the person of M. de Bonald, and ultra-liberalism in that of M. Benjamin Constant: the steady middle course of reason and practical good sense, to which it seems as if experience must bring us back at last!

And now, Sir, shall I say what most touches me in the works as in the life of my uncle?—what I recognize in him as far above poet or statesman, or, better still, what I find in both author and citizen, as the sap in the tree, the soul in the body? You have placed at the front of our dear volume the words which his illustrious friend, Victor Cousin, uttered over his coffin: "Thine has been a pure life and a Christian death. I must needs remember that this is the only eulogy thy pious modesty would suffer." I have before me a letter written by the Abbé de Frayssinous to the young poet's mother a few days after his death, which begins thus: "It was my office, dear Madam, to attend upon your son Charles in the illness which terminated in his death. I feel bound to say, for your comfort, that I was well pleased with the state of his mind, and that everything leads me to believe that God has received him in mercy." It was to the hands of M. de Frayssinous that he committed that translation of Tibullus, sacrificed by him to no vain scruple of conscience, but to a faith at once enlightened and profound;—a translation which would have won him literary glory, but which would have done the wrong of introducing into Christian literature what is out of place anywhere else than among the heathen.

The secret of such a life and such a death, is to be looked for in his cradle. A child of the people—of that people which has ever been faithful to sound and genuine popular traditions and instincts, he has himself shown us the double sanctuary of his education in his father's house and the parish church.

> "The humble shop where thirty years they toiled
> In poverty, to earn our daily bread."*
>
> * * * * * * *
>
> "O sacred place! With waxen light in hand,
> The mystic sign of innocence and love,
> Hither we children came when welcomed first
> By the old pastor's venerable lips,
> Unto the heavenly banquet." s†

But in order to come at a more intimate personal knowledge of his Christian faith, founded, as all true Christian faith is, on living demonstration rather than on discussions and theories, we must read a touching

---

* Voilà l'humble atelier où mes pauvres parents
Pour nourrir leur famille, ont travaillé trente ans.

* * * * * * *

Vois-tu ce lieu sacré ? C'est là qu'un cierge en main,
Signe mystérieux d'amour et d'innocence,
Pour la première fois au celeste festin,
Un pasteur vénérable accueillit notre enfance.
Les Souvenirs de l'Enfance.

poem addressed to his brother, which is entitled "The Service for the Dead, and a Visit to the Country Churchyard at our Birth-place." It is a genuine outburst of fraternal feeling, and although written in most elegant verse, shows the utter self-forgetfulness of a heart that has abandoned itself to the scene before it, and to the presentiment of approaching death. Amid these funereal forms, there comes into view the figure of a most sweet and Christian woman, an apparition from heaven, which the grave does but too speedily hide away from the childish vision, but which lingers still in memory to be the light of a whole lifetime. She was a peasant-woman of Brittany, his maternal grandmother, my own great-grandmother, who had already left the world when I entered it, but the charm of whose life was impressed upon my childhood, through the long stories, full of sober feeling, that my brother used to tell me.

> "I see her still, devout and diligent,
> In her old corner by the spacious hearth,
> Where the dull fire flung out its flickering light,
> From dawn to eve, spinning, and praying God."*

A simple but exalted spirit, a strong, though gentle soul, that had passed through the storm of the revolution with her light in her hand, or rather in her heart, without suffering it either to flicker or die out, Madame Lesue—permit my pen this once to rest upon her name—had bequeathed to her children far more than fortune or title; honest and vigorous blood, the faith of the Gospel, the virtues of family and Christian life.

* Toujours je crois la voir, pieuse et diligente,
Près du large foyer où brille un humble feu,
De l'aube jusqu'au soir filant et priant Dieu.

> "Seeds of salvation, motherly words and tones,
> Spring up, and cover all my life with fruit!
> To her whose hand first sowed you in my heart,
> I pledge undying gratitude and love."*

I pause at this aspiration, which was my uncle's and is mine, and close, with no small emotion, the story of that religious festival which took place in the depth of a country province, at Château Gontier, sixty years ago, and which I meet again, celebrated with so much of solemnity and of popular interest in this capital, which may sometimes appear to forget its God, but never its dead. These bells of the second of November have tears on their brazen cheeks, and sobs in their tones; but as I listen to them, even while I write these lines, I seem to hear in them the echo of the voice of Patmos:

"I heard a voice from heaven, saying unto me: write. Blessed are the dead who die in the Lord. Yea, saith the Spirit, that they may rest from their labors, and their works do follow them."

Brother Hyacinthe,
Barefooted Carmelite.

Paris, November 2, 1868.
   [All-Souls Day.]

---

* Salutaires leçons, préceptes maternels,
Croissez, et de vos fruits couvrez ma vie entière!
A celle dont la main vous sema la première,
Mon cœur a consacré des regrets immortels.

APPENDIX.

MEN AND PARTIES

IN THE CATHOLIC CHURCH IN FRANCE,

JUST BEFORE THE ŒCUMENICAL COUNCIL, 1869.

[The following is part of an Article by the Rev. Edward de Pressensé, in the Revue Chrétienne for September and October, 1869. The author of it is the foremost man of French Protestantism—a man of acknowledged fairness and ability, and held in high esteem by his fellow-citizens of the Roman Catholic faith.]

* * * It is important to bear in mind all along, that we are only just passed the *coup d'état* of December, when, with something of an explosion, a division took place in the Catholic camp. We have first a very original figure among the superior clergy; it is Monseigneur Dupanloup, bishop of Orleans. I know that for some years past he has been pardoned many of his old offences at Rome, in consideration of the impetuosity of his defence of the temporal power of the Pope. Always impetuous, of an effervescent temperament, with a quick, lively pen, he is a sort of Bohemian bishop, with a decided talent for controversy. The author of several approved works on education, he owes his reputation above all to his talent as a controversialist always in the breach. He has taken open issue with the *Univers*—seemingly, at first, on a merely literary question. A certain Abbé Gaume, since bishop, had taken it into his head to oppose classical studies, under the signature of *Ver Rongeur*. M. Dupanloup, a man of culture, a prelate destined to become a member of the Académie Française, stigmatized this barbarous obscurantism, which, withal, is no part of the Roman traditions. He has always taken sides with political liberty, so long as people refrained from the indiscretion of claiming it for Rome. We shall see shortly that the bishop of Orleans has verged very closely upon the party of violence, in the struggles of these last years. He is called something of a Gallican. It is pretty hard to see in what his Gallicanism consists. The Abbé Cœur, bishop of Troyes, since dead, Monseigneur Sibour, archbishop of Paris, who was struck by the dagger of an assassin at the very moment when he had instituted a prosecution against the *Univers* for its extravagant polemics, were men of like tendency.

Three men have especially made their mark in the Liberal-Catholic party First, the two old disciples of Lamennais, the Abbé Lacordaire and M. de Montalembert. The first had revived the festivals of high eloquence under the vault of Notre Dame. It was all very well to hold him in suspicion and at some distance on account of his association with Lamennais; but no sooner had he uttered his voice in the little chapel of Stanislas college, than his superb eloquence rang through Paris after such a fashion, that there was nothing else to be done, in spite of the monstrous outcries of bigotry, but to put him into the pulpit of the metropolitan church. Every precaution was taken. He was required to communicate in advance the plans of his discourses, but once abandoned to the passion of his inspiration, the torrent carried everything before it, and they looked in vain, the next day, in the archbishop's chancery, to detect in the fiery improvisation of the orator any trace of the plan that had been submitted and approved. He skirted along perilous gulfs without ever falling into them; but the spirit which animated him was altogether modern and liberal.

His favorite enterprise of reviving the Dominican Order in France, is well known. But his white monk's robe made only one more contrast with his wholly unclerical manner of thinking and speaking. His lectures at Notre Dame were open to serious criticism—the reasoning often bordered closely upon sophistry—more than once the logic is fanciful, and after all the essential elements of Catholic doctrine are preserved by him. But a glow of generous feeling pervades his whole discourse. Now and then it breaks out, and then the subdued, entranced audience feels that electric thrill which is the sign of true eloquence. On the very surface of his discourse there is always to be recognized an ardent love of liberty. On the day following the *coup d'état*, he expressed himself with such energy in a sermon preached at Paris, that all the pulpits of the city were thenceforth closed to the illustrious Dominican. His voice was never afterward heard, except in the addresses delivered at his reception into the Académie Française.

Since his death, which occurred in 1861, the public have been admitted to the secrets of his interior life. This brilliant orator, whose words stirred men's minds, sometimes, like those of a tribune of the people, was, in reality, a true monk in point of austerity. He subjected himself in secret to unheard-of macerations, which unquestionably shortened his life. He craved humiliation and suffering, and did not shrink before an asceticism which could hardly have been surpassed by a Hindoo fakeer. In his heart of hearts, Lacordaire suffered intensely from the inward struggle between the convictions of his youth, which responded to his deepest instincts, and his sincere but forced submission to the papacy. He profoundly felt that the spirit is above the letter, and that the inspirations which came forth from Rome were not those which animated either his soul or his speech.

M. de Montalembert was the worthy rival and the faithful friend of the great Dominican preacher.

By nature more excitable and impressible, he had more difficulty in ridding himself of the powerful ties which bound him to Lamennais; but then, for a time, the rupture was more radical. There has even been one phase in which he seemed to prefer the church above liberty. It was during the violent reaction which followed the revolution of 1848. The attitude which he held on the eve of the events of 1851, was not consistent with his previous record. Horror of demagogism inclined him for the moment toward Cesarism; but how grandly has he recovered himself from this defection! With what magnificent eloquence he has launched his thunderbolts against absolutism and all its props, most of all against those which were nearest to himself, and which dishonored Catholicism by their unworthy alliance! A sincere Christian, always impassioned and vehement, he has returned to his true flag, and we shall see with what courage he has known how to flout it in the face of the most obstinate prejudices. The Anglo-Saxon race has no more enthusiastic or enlightened admirer than this Catholic nobleman.

The third leader of the Liberal-Catholic party in 1852 was a young professor of the Sorbonne, M. Frédéric Ozanam, snatched away from a most brilliant career by consumption before he was forty years of age. He had the unspeakable advantage of being in constant relation with the youth of the university by means of his course of instruction in foreign literature, rich, as it was, in research and eloquence. At the same time, he was one of the founders of the Society of Saint Vincent de Paul,—a society of laymen, designed for the visitation of the poor, and also to form among young Catholics a bond of active charity. Ozanam united the finest endowments of intellect with admirable piety. Already sick and emaciated, he was seen climbing the staircases of tenement houses to carry to the poor both material aid and words of sympathy. Owing to his influence, the association had rapidly increased, and from the start was animated by the purest charity. Ozanam possessed all the most generous passions of youth, and, foremost of all, the love of liberty. He, too, dreamed of bringing about an alliance between his most cherished belief in humanity and his religious faith. This thought was the very soul of his teaching, which achieved a very distinguished success at the Sorbonne by the soundness of its erudition, and the somewhat feverish brilliancy of an eloquence which was wearing away his life. He used some expressions of extraordinary boldness, such as this: "There are some persons who believe in their God only when he walks in a purple robe."—"No, no," said he at another time, "I do not believe that fire has ever had power to conquer an idea, however false and detestable it might be."

Nothing can be more touching than the resignation of M. Ozanam, when he found that he must give up in early manhood all that gave life its value—the purest domestic happiness, a most noble and useful career, a most brilliant future. I know nothing more admirable than the story of his death, as told by Father Lacordaire.

Among the men holding the same views, we may mention the Prince de Broglie, the illustrious representative of one of the most distinguished families in France. Grandson of Madame de Staël, son of that Duke de Broglie who was one of the purest and strongest types of the liberal and Christian statesman, the inflexible upholder of justice, M. A. de Broglie has nobly sustained this formidable inheritance. An eminent historian of the Church of the fourth century, his talent is never more conspicuous than in religious or political controversy. He brings to that work a lofty irony which gives to his eloquence a singularly incisive character. It is evident that he has not breathed the stormy atmosphere of the school of Lamennais. Liberty has come to him as an undisputed heir-loom. He lays claim to it with less of passion, and sometimes with less of breadth than M. de Montalembert, but, withal, is not in the least liable to the reproach of any political inconsistency.

As for the liberalism of M. de Falloux, he holds it neither by family tradition, nor through the Lamennaisian apostolical succession. By nature, by association, he belongs to the purest legitimism. He wrote the life of Pius V., the Inquisitor, and declared in that book that tolerance is the virtue of the unbelieving ages. We should hardly look, then, to find in him a liberal from conviction. Nevertheless, after the *coup d'état*, he made a clean breach with absolutist Catholicism, and took rank among the defenders of public liberty. The *Correspondant*, a monthly magazine, has become the organ of this great Liberal-Catholic party, and its remarkable success is due to him.

We must not forget the very interesting group of the new French Oratory, revived by Father Gratry, the amiable and sympathetic defender of modern Christianity, who mixes up a little too much the differential calculus with moral demonstration, but who is always eloquent, lofty, broad, deeply enamored of liberty, though too indulgent toward the Jesuit order ;. a liberal nature, desirous of reconciling the irreconcilable in theory and practice.

Let us single out again, outside of and above these two distinct parties, an eminent man, M. Arnaud de l'Ariége, who has represented democratic ideas in our republican meetings with admirable ability, associating them with profoundly Christian convictions. Already at this time, he had far outgone the liberal party of the Catholic Church in openly demanding the complete separation of Church and State, as a first condition of the highest development of the individual by a truly personal faith.

Gallicanism, properly so called, was revived several years ago, forming a third party, insignificant in point of numbers, but which counted some very distinguished adherents. The Abbé Guettée, a learned historian of the Church of France, had sought to find in national traditions some firm ground for resistance to Ultramontanism. His heavy and awkwardly-written book was a well-furnished arsenal against Rome. To the same party belonged no less decidedly an eminent theologian, the Abbé Maret, professor of theology in the faculty of Paris, known by his works of solid value against pantheism and against the traditionalist school, as it is called, which, in order better to establish the authority of the Church, overturned all rational foundations of the truth in man. The Abbé Maret, although an orthodox Catholic, was opposed to the exaggerated pretensions of the papacy, and showed himself more concerned about the ancient rights of the Church of France than the Abbé Lacordaire, with whom, nevertheless, he united in starting "The New Era" (*L'Ere Nouvelle*), in 1848. The Holy See has never forgiven him this spirit of independence, for it has shown a very ill grace in confirming his nomination to a bishopric "*in partibus.*" It was pretended that he was growing deaf. And, in point of fact, he did seem to be a little hard of hearing when called upon to listen to instructions from the court of Rome. This was in their eyes an incurable malady. But that wing of the Gallican party which was most openly accused and most distinctively liberal, was shut up within the narrow attic of a hermit-philosopher, M. Bordas Demoulin, known by his admirable philosophic works upon Descartes. With his disciple, M. Huet, he constituted the entire school; but it made up for its numerical feebleness by the indomitable energy, the courageous faith of its head. M. Bordas Demoulin lived in retirement and poverty, not willing in any way to compromise his proud independence, uttering imprecations like an indignant prophet against the humiliation of the Church, and declaring emphatically that all was over with her if she failed to ally herself openly with democracy. He insisted above all upon her duty of breaking off all connection with temporal powers, in order to begin again with a wooden cross in her hands and a word of liberty on her lips, the conquest of a world which is slipping out of her hold. M. Bordas Demoulin has developed these great thoughts in his book on "The Constituent Powers of the Church" (*Des Pouvoirs constituants de l'Eglise*), in which he has set forth his whole system. M. Huet has given these ideas greater publicity by means of short and sprightly papers animated by the same stern and liberal spirit. The school of M. Bordas Demoulin will certainly always be considered one of the most interesting and honorable manifestations of the time.

Such was the situation of minds in the Catholic Church of France on the morrow of the *coup d'état* of December, and in part under the influence of those gloomy events. We are acquainted now with its principal parties, and the men who play a controlling part in them. We are prepared to understand the troubles and conflicts which are to be provoked, in coming years, by the decisions into which the court of Rome has allowed itself to be drawn.

The first of these decisions was the proclamation of the dogma of the Immaculate Conception, in 1854. It is altogether unnecessary to emphasize the gravity of this audacious stroke of the papacy. However important in itself might be the doctrinal decision which would promote beyond measure the tendency toward Mariolatry, the fact that it had dared to promulgate a dogma without the sanction of a council, was the most dangerous and insolent of the innovations of ultra montanism. Never had anything been seen like it. Always in the past there had been reserved to the Church, regularly represented, the important right of the definition of doctrine. But nothing could be more unlike a regular council than the consultation by letter of the principal bishops, and the hasty meeting of a certain number of them at Rome. In another age, less ignorant than ours in a religious point of view, so daring an attempt of the papacy would have set fire to the four corners of the earth; or rather, the fear of public opinion would have put any such project out of the question. The *Gesù* (the centre of the Jesuit order) at Rome well knew that it need have no fear of making any considerable disturbance in men's minds by an attempt which nevertheless surpassed everything of the sort which had ever before been seen. The rejoicing was immense in the camp of the fanatical adherents of the Pope. The party of the *Univers* climbed the Capitoline and intoned the "*Nunc dimittis.*" It had, in truth, seen the dawn of the day so glorious for that party, of the absolute subjugation of the Church. The most liberal wing of the ultra montanists had no scruple in receiving the new dogma with acclamations. The *Correspondant* joined in chorus with the *Univers*, and the Abbé Gratry outdid all others in exalting the Immaculate Conception of Mary. It was only the old Gallicanism that felt itself struck to the heart. The men eminent by position whom it counted within its ranks confined themselves to silent lamentations; but we know how bitter and melancholy were those days to many among them. MM. Bordas Demoulin and Huet uttered an energetic protest. In a book entitled "An Essay upon Catholic Reformation" (*Essai sur la reforme catholique*), they showed how ancient tradition had been trodden under foot by the Jesuits of Rome. "What a crime," cried M. Huet, "to throw itself across the path of this perpetual succession of truth! Above all, what a crime on the part of those whose prime mission it is to teach the truth—who have solemnly sworn to defend it!" These courageous opponents have no hesitation in charging the new dogma with heresy. "As it includes," say they, " all corruptions, so it leads inevitably to the demand for radical and complete reformation. The time allows neither compromise nor delay. When open attack made upon the revelation of God is manifest, submission is not obedience, but apostasy, and renunciation of the Christian faith." MM. Bordas Demoulin and Huet said aloud what was thought or muttered by many others.

The most energetic protest was that of an old priest, the Abbé Laborde, a man universally respected, who, on the announcement of what was preparing at Rome, started for the centre of Catholicity, imagining, in his simplicity, that the voice of truth would get a hearing among the princes of the Church, even though its mouthpiece were only a humble country vicar. He carried to the Pope a brief and forcible paper, entitled " The Belief in the Immaculate Conception cannot become a Dogma of Faith" (*La croyance à l'Immaculée Conception ne peut devenir un dogme de foi*). The story is well worth reading, of the persecutions to which he was subjected by the papal police. Hunted as a criminal, he was at last shipped for France by violence, and returned thither to die on a hospital pallet, where, with his dying hand, he finished a last protest against the new errors. It is a light thing that the righteous man's complaint is unheeded on the earth—it has been heard in heaven; and the sentence pronounced by him on his deathbed against the usurpations of the papacy, is confirmed by God himself: it shall not be annulled.

Political events, in their swift progress, have come up to involve the internal crisis of Catholicism in singular complications. The gravest of these events was the war in Italy, which prostrated in the Peninsula the power of Austria, the natural protector of the papacy. The latter, speedily bereft of some of its fairest provinces, menaced in the possession of the rest, that were still struggling under its yoke, naturally took the most violent attitude toward the new kingdom of Italy, which it had openly excommunicated. The old-style politics took on, in its eyes, a character of actual sanctity as being the only thing that gave any promise of maintaining the temporal power. This explains the fact that after the Italian war in 1859, reactionary principles found more favor than ever at Rome, and that hatred of civil and religious liberty were there carried to the point of actual fanaticism. Absolutism of all sorts is the bulwark of the temporal power of the Pope, which can be maintained on no other ground.

It is easy now for us to understand in what way the Holy See has been led to the Encyclical of December, 1864, and the appended "Syllabus." It certainly would never have let itself be dragged into these acts of unmitigated folly, unless it had believed itself to be in a state of permanent aggressive war. Every advance of liberty seemed to it to knock one stone out of the wall behind which it is defending its political sovereignty. Accordingly it runs a-tilt against it, as a mortal enemy, even when liberalism shows itself most careful not to hurt it, and halts before the temporal power, as if it had come to a reserved region which must be an exception to all the general principles of modern society. The *Correspondant* has had some little experience of this. The Pope is in the right about it. The logic of events will not always stop short just where we would like to have it. With the best disposition in the world to stop half-way in the argument, we don't more than half succeed. It is not possible to advocate the cause of liberty at Paris and oppose it at Rome. We cannot go on saying "true this side the Alps, false the other side." Liberal Catholicism, whether it will or no, is listed in the grand crusade against pontifical absolutism, and in the long siege which will end with throwing down the wall of this European China. These considerations explain the internal conflicts of Catholicism, and the condemnations which have been obtained against its most illustrious champions. It is because, with all their attempts to disguise or defend the abuses of the temporal papacy, they are doing it less good, than they are damaging it by their general advocacy of liberty.

Nevertheless, the Catholics of the *Correspondant* do not spare their strength in the defence of the temporal power. Instead of being content with inflicting on the Italian administrations the reproaches that have been justly deserved by their tortuous and often Machiavellian policy, they have poured out their spleen on Italy itself, simply on the ground that it had laid hands on the property of the Lord's anointed. In their journals, they turned against it their most impassioned polemics, without once being willing to consider what mischief it had suffered from that papal power which had been the everlasting hindrance to its enfranchisement, and which never ceased to wish it every possible annoyance. When M. de Cavour accepted as his own motto one of the finest expressions of Montalembert, " A free Church in a free State," the Liberal-Catholic party were almost ready to cry out, Blasphemy! Orators, journalists, bishops, all vied with each other in denouncing the Italian nation, and insulting its aspirations. It was a question between the Bishop of Orleans and his colleague of Poitiers, which should do most to roll Italy in the mud, and to magnify the beauty, the gentleness, the liberality of the pontifical government. The *Correspondant* party did more than devote its pen to the cause of the temporal power; it furnished to it its most illustrious sword in the person of General Lamoricière, the vanquished of Castelfidardo. There was only one solitary voice in the Catholic camp that did not join in chorus with the defenders of the priest-king. This was the voice of M. Arnaud de l'Ariége, who published in 1868 a book entitled *Italy*, in which he protested, in the name of religion, against this fatal confounding of faith and politics. We cannot refrain from citing from it the following fragment, which, in the midst of the theocratic fever, vindicates the honor and the tradition of Christian spirituality.

" Whenever, at any point in the civilized world, a grave attack is aimed at the rights of conscience, all consciences feel the bond of common interest, and there breaks forth at once a universal protest.

" Let but a Jewish child, at Rome, be snatched from its family by fanatical priests, and every friend of justice, Rationalist, or

Protestant, or Catholic, forgets his religious party in thinking of the rights of the outraged father. Let dissenting Christians in Spain be condemned by the secular courts for their acts of worship, and the Universal Israelite Alliance lifts up, in favor of its Christian brethren, the most noble and touching remonstrances.

"Is Rome alone, in this concert of civilized nations, to be wanting to its mission? When liberty is the first need of the age—a need so imperative that even those who curse it at the bottom of their hearts are compelled to assume the disguise of it—when it is the star toward which are turned the eyes of the oppressed of the whole earth, is the temporal Rome of the popes to remain the insurmountable obstacle to it? This state of things, which holds Italy and all Christendom in check, is a vast misfortune, and almost a defiance flung by the spirit of the past before the aspirations of the civilized world.

"No event, therefore, occurring in Europe, can be sufficient to justify us in losing sight of this great interest, which overtops all others in importance. Keep it ever before the people—every liberal conquest will be precarious, every solution will be incomplete, so long as the knot is not fairly cut at Rome by the abolition of the temporal papacy. For years past, therefore, we have made this our *Delenda Carthago*.

"Furthermore, every institution has got to be tested by liberty. The obstinacy of the Catholic clergy, in clinging to a political basis, convinces only too many of the men of liberal sentiments that the Church has no other foundation, and that when this foundation fails, the whole structure will tumble at once."

Such language as this could not but be displeasing at Rome: but then, on the other hand, the papal power was bound to show its gratitude to those eminent men who had undertaken to be its champions. But it accorded this cordially and unreservedly, only to those who had served it exactly according to its mind, and had understood distinctly that the cause of the papal power was identical with the cause of absolutism. It dreaded the support of liberal Catholics, because it perceived clearly enough that the breath which animated them was not its own spirit, and that it was the same breath which had first roused Italy, and then sustained her in opposition to Rome. It understood clearly that it is not possible long to eulogize civil liberty, and, above all, liberty of conscience, in all countries, and proscribe them at one solitary point in the universe. Thus the instinct of self-preservation rendered it more perspicacious and logical than those pious knights of Catholic liberalism, who, burning with incompatible ardors, devoted themselves at once to the temporal power of the Pope and to liberty. It was inevitable but that this misunderstanding should be speedily cleared up, and nothing tended more to precipitate an open rupture between the parties, than the grand liberal manifestation that took place at the Catholic congress of Malines, in August, 1863. It was the former disciple of Lamennais, M. de Montalembert, who took the initiative, with accents which strikingly recalled that fiery old man, the editor of the *Avenir*. Everybody ought to read, entire, his two speeches of August 21 and 23, 1863. They were afterward printed as a pamphlet, and are a splendidly eloquent summary of all the principles of liberal Catholicism without forgetting its inconsistencies. In these impassioned harangues, Montalembert reclaims his share in the estate bequeathed by Cavour, and develops anew the famous motto, "A free Church in a free State." He starts, to be sure, with making his disclaimers. He calls that illustrious minister who was the founder of Italian unity, a great criminal. He labors with no small trouble to show how his ideas of the perfect independence of the church are capable of being reconciled with the Roman theocracy, and how (to use the standard phrase) the two powers have to be united at Rome, in order that they may be separated everywhere else. But all these concessions, which he makes with perfect sincerity, only give the stronger emphasis to his energetic enforcement of the claims of liberty. He declares boldly that he has no tears for past institutions—that the church must resolutely turn its back upon the old order of things, and fall in, loyally, with the great liberties of modern times—the liberty of universal suffrage, of association, of the press, and of worship. In order to clear up all misunderstanding, the great orator devotes his whole speech to this last liberty. Let him speak for himself. We shall see, a little further on, what importance this passage has in the history of contemporary Catholicism:

"Of all the liberties which I have undertaken to defend, the most precious, in my view, the most sacred, the most legitimate, the most necessary, is liberty of conscience. I have loved and served all forms of human liberty; but I claim the special honor of having been a champion of this. Even now, after so many a struggle, and so many a defeat, I cannot speak of it without unwonted emotion. Yes, we are bound to love and serve all liberties, but among them all, the tenderest respect, the most absolute devotion is due to religious liberty; for this it is which soars in regions the loftiest and purest, and at the same time, the most vast. Its domain stretches from the depths of the individual conscience to the most splendid manifestations of national life. This alone illuminates two lives and two worlds: the life of the soul as well as of the body; heaven as well as earth. This, alone, is of equal importance to all men without exception—poor and rich, strong and weak, people and kings, the least of our little ones, and the intellect of a Newton or a Leibnitz.

"And yet—most strange and grievous thing!—it is this liberty, the most delicate, the most exposed of all, which one cannot handle without crushing it—it is this which, everywhere proclaimed in theory, is almost everywhere, in fact, least understood, least respected, least protected from a thousand rude or treacherous attacks, too often unnoticed or unpunished.

"I must confess that this enthusiastic devotion of mine to religious liberty, is not general among Catholics. They are very fond of it for themselves—which is no great merit. Generally speaking, everybody likes every sort of liberty for himself. But religious liberty for its own sake, the liberty of other men's consciences, the liberty of worship which men denounce and repudiate—this is what disturbs and enrages many of us.

"I go for liberty of conscience, in the interest of Catholicism, without reservation and without hesitation. I frankly accept all those consequences of it which equity requires and public morality does not forbid. This brings me to a delicate but essential question. I come to it without circumlocution, because in all discussions of this sort, I have always found the importance of meeting in advance the very natural and often very sincere anxiety which obtains among the enemies of the liberty of Catholics. Are we at liberty, now-a-days, to demand liberty for the truth—that is, for ourselves (for every honest man believes what he holds to be the truth), and refuse it to error—that is, to persons who differ from us?

"I answer flatly—no. I am well aware that I am treading, here, on dangerous ground. *Incedo per ignes*. I hasten, accordingly, to repeat that I make no pretence to express anything more than an individual opinion. I bow before all the texts and all the canons that will be quoted against me. I shall neither dispute them nor discuss them. But I cannot crush out the conviction of my conscience and heart. I cannot do otherwise than express it, now that I have read, for twelve years past, those essays on the restoration of men and things to a perfect state, which nobody, when I was a young man—at least no Catholic—ever thought of defending. I declare, therefore, that I feel an invincible horror at all punishments and all violences inflicted on mankind under pretence of serving or defending religion. The fagots lighted by the hands of Catholics, are as horrible to me as the scaffolds on which Protestants have immolated so many martyrs. [*Sensation and applause.*] The gag in the mouth of any sincere preacher of his own faith, I feel as if it were between my own lips, and it makes me shudder with distress. [*Renewed sensation.*] The Spanish inquisitor, saying to the heretic, "The truth, or death," is as odious to me as the French terrorist saying to my grandfather, "Liberty and fraternity, or death." [*Shouts of applause.*] The human conscience has the right to demand that none of these hideous alternatives shall ever be imposed on it." [*Renewed applause.*]

Such language as this certainly left nothing to be desired in point of precision. Received with enthusiasm in the Liberal-Catholic party (although it must have appeared extravagant to some of them), in the opposite party it waked up a lively indignation, especially in the burning centre of Roman Jesuitism; for M. de Montalembert had laid an audacious hand on the fundamental principles of that powerful body, and on the very basis of their private teaching. We are compelled to believe that it was just after the congress of Malines, and as a sequel to all the protests and denunciations to which that congress gave rise, that the Encyclical of December 8th, 1864, was prepared. Read it without prejudice, giving its words their natural sense, and it is not possible to help seeing in it the clearest refutation of all that Montalembert had declared, with a generous passion, on the platform of the congress:

"Ye are not ignorant, venerable brethren, that there are not wanting, at this day, men who, applying to civil society the impious and absurd principle of *naturalism*, as they call it, make bold to teach that the perfection of government and the progress of States demand that society be constituted and governed without taking any more account of religion than if there were no such thing, or at least without making any discrimination be tween the true religion and the false. Furthermore, contrary to the doctrine of the Scripture, the Church, and the holy Fathers, they do not hesitate to declare that the best government is that in which no obligation is recognized in the authorities to repress by legal penalties the violators of the Catholic faith, except so far as the interests of the public peace demand. Setting out with this absolutely false conception of government, they do not stick at encouraging that erroneous opinion, fatal to the Catholic Church, and to the salvation of souls, which our predecessor, Gregory XVI., of happy memory, characterized as a *delirium*, that liberty of conscience and of worship is a right which belongs to every man, and which ought to be proclaimed by law, and protected in every well-constituted State; and that citizens have a right to the full liberty of manifesting their opinions, whether it may be by speech, by printing, or otherwise, without any power of restriction on the part either of the ecclesiastical or of the civil authority. Now in maintaining these rash declarations, they neither think nor consider that they are preaching the liberty of perdition, and that if it is always permitted to human opinions to dispute everything, there will never be wanting those who will dare to resist the truth, and put confidence in the words of man's reason—a most mischievous vanity which Christian faith and wisdom must carefully avoid, according to the instruction of our Lord Jesus Christ himself.

"And since wherever religion is banished from civil society, and the doctrine and authority of the divine revelation rejected, the true notion even of human justice and duty becomes obscured and lost, and material force takes the place of true justice and lawful right, it is precisely on this account that certain men, making no account of the most settled principles of sound reason, dare to proclaim that the will of the people, manifested by what they call public opinion, or in some other way, constitutes the supreme law, independent of all right, divine and human, and that in political affairs, established facts, by the very fact of their being established, have the force of right.

"Now, who does not see, who does not feel distinctly, that Society, withdrawn from the laws of religion and true righteousness, can have no other object than that of heaping up riches, and in all its doings will follow no other law than the indomitable desire to satisfy its passions and serve its interests? Therefore, men of this sort persecute with cruel hatred the religious orders, making no account of the immense services which they have rendered to religion, society, and literature. They cry out against them, saying that they have no legitimate reason for existing, and thus they become the echo of the calumnies of heretics. In effect, as it was very wisely said by Pius VII., our predecessor of happy memory, ' the abolition of the religious orders is a blow at the liberty of publicly practising the gospel teachings; it is a blow at a manner of life recommended by the Church as conformed to the apostles' doctrine; finally, it is a blow at those illustrious founders whom we venerate at the altar, and who did not establish these orders except by the inspiration of God!'

"They go further yet, and declare in their impiety that it is necessary to take away from the faithful and the Church the right of doing alms publicly in the name of Christian charity, and to abolish the law which forbids servile labor on certain days in order to make room for divine worship: and this under the most false pretext that this right and this law are inconsistent with the principles of sound public economy.

"Not content with banishing religion from society, they would fain exclude it even from the bosom of the family. Teaching and professing the fatal error of communism and socialism, they affirm that domestic society, or the family, has the ground of its existence purely in civil law; and consequently that all the rights of parents over children, and especially the right to instruct and educate, are derived from the civil law and dependent on it. With these men of falsehood, the principal object of these impious maxims and these machinations, is to withdraw completely from the salutary doctrine and influence of the Church the instruction and education of youth, in order to defile and deprave, by the most pernicious errors, and by every sort of vice, the tender and flexible soul of the young. In effect, all those who have undertaken the overthrow of religious and social order, and to bring to naught all laws, divine and human, have always and above all combined their plans, their actions, and their efforts, for the deception and perversion of the youth, because, as we have already indicated, they put all their hope in the corruption of the rising generation.

"Neglect not, also, to teach that royal power is conferred, not only for the government of this world, but, above all, for the protection of the Church; and that nothing can be more for the advantage and glory of chief magistrates and kings than to conform themselves to the words which our most wise and courageous predecessor, St. Felix, wrote to the Emperor Zeno, that he should leave the Church free to govern itself by its own laws, and suffer no man to interfere with its liberty.... It is unquestionably for their interest, in all matters that concern the things of God, carefully to follow the order which he has laid down, and to set the royal will below, and not above, the will of the priests of Christ."

Among the propositions condemned by the "*Syllabus*" which follows the Encyclical are the following:

"That every man is free to embrace and profess that religion which he regards as true, according to the light of his reason."

"IV. 24. That the Church has not the power of using force; that she has no power, direct or indirect."

"54. That the Church ought to be separated from the State, and the State from the Church."

"74. That matrimonial cases belong to the jurisdiction of the civil State."

"77. That, in our times, it is no longer expedient that the Catholic religion should be considered as the only religion of the State, to the exclusion of all other religions.

"78. That accordingly, in some Catholic countries, it has very properly been provided by law that immigrants should enjoy the public exercise of their respective religions.

"79. That it is false that civil liberty granted to all religions propagates the plague of indifferentism.

"80. That the Roman pontiff can and ought to be reconciled and come into harmony with progress, liberalism, and modern civilization."

These are (don't mistake it) not the things approved, but the things condemned.

Now, let us consider the effect of this document on the three parties of Catholicism in France—absolutist ultramontanism, liberal ultramontanism, and Gallicanism in its various shades more or less distinctly marked. There is no need of inquiring concerning the first party. Its answer is known beforehand. Its shouts had all the insolence of triumph and revenge. The two newspapers, the *Univers* and the *Monde*, abused without stint the advantage they had gained. They saw the sacred shield of infallibility stretched out over their favorite doctrines, and over that whole system of civil and religious tyranny which they never tired of preaching up. The Head of the Church, in fact, declared that they alone had truly known his mind, and that the apologists of the Inquisition and the dragonnades were the real organs of eternal truth.

The second party, the liberal Catholicism of the *Correspondant*, at first bent its head before the storm, all the time inwardly gnawing at its bonds. The pontifical condemnation struck it fairly between the eyes. It is enough to put the Encyclical alongside of the manifesto of M. de Montalembert at Malines. Either human language has ceased to be the equivalent of the thoughts it undertakes to express, or the contradiction between these two documents is just as clear as it could be. The *Correspondant* party ought to have continued its attitude of silence. After all, an encyclical is not a dogma; it tolerates a mental reservation. Unluckily the bishop of Orleans did not see his way to practise the part of prudence, which was also the part of dignity. Vexed at seeing what a handle the enemies of the Church were making of the Encyclical, he wrote a pamphlet to show that it was all right, that what the holy father had been condemning was license, not liberty. With a diversion from the main question which showed no little smartness, the fiery prelate began with dashing head first into political controversy, discussing in an excited way the convention of September 15, 1864, between France and Italy, according to which, the French occupation of Rome was to be promptly ended. After firing hot shot against a treaty which he deemed a treason, he approached the Encyclical, and went into a thousand subtleties of interpretation to show that there was a hidden meaning, and a reasonable one, in the holy father's anathemas. It was sewing new cloth on the old garment of the Vatican, and making the rent worse, as the Gospel said. No ingenuity of interpretation could hide the deplorable explicitness of the text. All his nice distinctions could not prevent the world from seeing that the blow was aimed directly against my lord of Orleans and his friends. Everybody knew that his party had moved heaven and earth to prevent the Encyclical from coming out. To undertake, at this time of day, to show that it had been got up expressly to please them, was one of those bold manœuvres which demand such an excessive amount of dexterity that they become actually clumsy. Montalembert was careful enough to keep out of this track. He kept quiet for awhile, and then went on and developed exactly the same thoughts and sentiments as in the past, just as if the Encyclical had never appeared. One may see how incorrigible he was, by reading those fine pages which he devoted to the American war, and which gave him the opportunity of renewing his homage to the great Anglo-Saxon race, and to political and religious liberty. O impotence of official authority in the sphere of intellect and morals! the very men who most respect it, treat it as if it had no existence!

For all this, the Encyclical troubled a great many honest consciences. We have a most remarkable proof of this in a book which the *Correspondant* did not venture to announce, although it was written by one of its contributors, M. de Metz-Noblat, an earnest Catholic, a broad and elevated mind, who exerts a great influence in the well-known group of liberals at Nancy. The title of the book is "Church and State." It is a collection of articles on the great question of the relation between the temporal and the spiritual powers. The author inclines perceptibly toward separation, without pronouncing a perfectly decided opinion. He winds up his book with a very grave declaration, which is more than a simple expression of his ideas—it is the very trouble of his conscience, which he reveals to us, in view of the follies of the Roman Curia. He is aware that he is not speaking only for himself, but that his troubles and misgivings are shared by all those

Catholics who decline to sell out their most earnest convictions. Hence the importance of this noble and loyal protest:

"What are the resources of that cohort of zealots who are laboring to realize, sooner or later, the subordination of the temporal power to the spiritual, and the indirect reign of the Church over the nations? If they attempt to carry their point by main force, they will fall at the first step upon insurmountable obstacles. Can they overcome them to-day? No. They are not able to hold the very ground they already occupy. Well; the day after a dogmatic decision, the obstacles will be greater yet; and they will have fewer allies, fewer auxiliaries, fewer soldiers, perhaps: they will be more watched, more hampered, more attacked. From that time, their best weapon will be cunning. They will find themselves reduced (it is so, from this day forth) to demanding liberty for the Church in the name of justice, in the name of equal rights—hiding their inner thoughts and ulterior intentions. They will have to conceal their object, in order to accomplish it. Vain subtlety! They will only lose honor, without achieving success. The trick is discovered. By the hundred tongues of the press it will be exposed and baffled. This is already the way with it, in some measure. How will it be, when no man shall be able to say, 'I am a Catholic, and nevertheless I do not aspire to establish the domination of the Church over the State?'

"To weaken the cause of the liberty of the Church, to strengthen the camp of its adversaries—such would infallibly be the consequences of erecting into dogmas those opinions to which the Encyclical, *Quanta cura*, restores, we cannot disguise it, a part of the authority which they had lost. Let us hope that things will go no further, and that an obligatory definition will not aggravate the embarrassments of a situation already sufficiently difficult."

The effect of the Encyclical was very considerable in the Gallican division of the Church. All the eminent men who belonged to it were wounded to the heart; but their characteristic doctrine of the non-infallibility of the Holy Father, so long as he speaks in his own name, suffered them to consider the Encyclical as a mere Roman manifesto, deplorable enough, no doubt, but not binding on the conscience. But it would have been very desirable to have this distinction set forth with a good deal of emphasis, in order to neutralize the unhappy effect of these pontifical declarations; for the effect of them had been immense. The French government had hit upon a notable plan for giving them the utmost possible notoriety, which was, to prohibit the official publication of them, on the ground that they conflicted with the rights of the nation. This interdict, coming after the press, with its thousand voices, had scattered the Encyclical in every direction, served only to interest liberal sentiment in favor of a document by which that sentiment was condemned in the most frantic strain. The State, by putting its big hand into this business, took the surest means of turning it into a muddle and a quibble.

To one of the most eminent representatives of liberal Gallicanism the Encyclical was the last drop in a full cup. M. Huet, who had stood alone in the breach since the death of M. Bordas Demoulin, had had no small trouble in keeping up any sort of concord between his bold liberalism and the Catholic Church. This concord became wholly impossible when the Pope had openly quarrelled with modern society with a frankness and audacity which surpassed everything of the sort that had thus far been seen. Unfortunately, M. Huet suffered the reaction to which he gave himself up, to carry him beyond Christianity itself, and enlisted into the ranks of the enemies of revelation, as may be easily seen by that deeply interesting book in which he recounts the history of his course of thought, under the title, "The Religious Revolution of the Nineteenth Century."

"Our age has known only one Catholic who could be called liberal, in the sense in which this title is given to the modern reformers of Protestantism and Judaism. This Catholic was Bordas. He was a man to resist the successors of Peter face to face. He conceived the bold design, over the ruins of existing abuses, of restoring to the various orders of the Church, the laity included, the primitive Christian liberty. But the event has only too well proved that Bordas was living after his time. He ought to have been born in the sixteenth century. He died a Catholic in name : in reality he was the truest and most thorough Protestant of his age.

"Three events of immense weight and scope have marked the reign of Pius IX., and have given over Catholicism irretrievably to ultramontane domination: the definition of the dogma of the Immaculate Conception in 1854, the Austrian concordat of 1855, and the Encyclical of 1864. These acts shut up Catholicism in a circle from which there is no escape.

"We are not now discussing theology; we are giving the history of a religious movement. In this view, the proclamation of the Immaculate Conception seems to us the most important fact in the annals of Catholicism for more than a century. Nothing but absolute indifference as to the result, or the absolute certainty of success among our contemporaries, could have caused the event to pass almost without notice. Nevertheless, let us remember the date of the eighth of December, 1854. It marks the advent of a new Catholicism, which we may term ultra-Catholicism, from which the spirit of the age and modern society can hope for neither truce nor mercy.

"As to the manner of proceeding, care was taken that the rival power to the papacy, the episcopacy, should find itself not only nullified but vilified—which is the most irreparable sort of destruction. They had an eye to this when they invited to Rome two hundred bishops. All deliberation was forbidden them, and there they stood by, dumb and smiling, at the most solemn act of Catholic life, the definition of a dogma. From that hour they descended from the authority of pastors to the level of the flock, and the everlasting ambition of Rome was satisfied. The infallibility of the Pope, which France had run aground for centuries, was under full headway amid the applauses of the Catholic world. The theocracy of Gregory VII. was revived with greater authority. The doctrinal and political consequences of it have not been slow in following, and the future will completely develop them.

"I know there are worthy members of the clergy who blame, and groan, and hope in secret. But is it possible for Catholicism to go backward? At the point where it is now fighting, the Church has, so to speak, burned its boats. All hope of reformation is lost.

"The teeming movement of modern life is sundering itself from the old counter-revolutionary Church, frozen stiff by ultramontane dogma. In that Church superstition is spreading wide its reign, having no congenial ally but the subtleties of scholastic and rabbinic science. Bordas predicted what would be the fate of Catholicism if it should persist in reconstructing itself. It will be found, he said, to degenerate into paganism. The prophecy is coming true. The Neo-Catholicism or Marianism has made itself dogmatically incompatible with scientific progress, as well as with political and social progress. Loosing itself from the enlightened classes, it will become the religion of the country people, where it will die out like the first Roman paganism. Some choice spirits, beguiled by prejudices of habit or education, some old-fashioned metaphysicians may still take shelter under the shadow of the old sanctuary; for the masses, the springs of intellectual and moral life are dried up in that quarter. The reign of Pius IX. will mark the fatal date of the last decadence."

Such was the effect of the Encyclical upon one honest and earnest man. There is weighty instruction in it. M. Huet has just been taken away from his multitude of friends, attended by their most affectionate respect; for one had only to know him, to admire his firm love of justice and liberty.

It seems as if the giddy infatuation which drove the papacy to this act of folly, had at one moment infected the whole Catholic church of France. In the year 1868, it undertook the most deplorable campaign—the best adapted to multiply defections like that of M. Huet. The Peter the Hermit of this crusade was the indefatigable Bishop of Orleans, whose zeal is truly formidable—to his friends. The occasion of these new attacks upon the system of public education, was a very innocent innovation on the part of the Minister of Public Instruction, who, in order to encourage the education of girls, brought within their reach, in the principal cities of France, excellent courses of instruction by the professors of our Lyceums. There is really nothing so very terrible in such an arrangement. Mothers are free to send or not to send their daughters to these Lectures, which, withal, are absolutely neutral in a religious point of view. But the Church does not so understand it. It regards female education as its own property—its private estate. To interfere with it, it regards as an actual attack upon itself, an odious usurpation of power. This is what Monseigneur Dupanloup felt profoundly. So he multiplied pamphlet upon pamphlet, to denounce the foul conspiracy for giving secular instruction to girls, who ought, as he expressed it, to be reared in the lap of the Church. His cry of alarm was heard. The edicts of his colleagues followed upon his call, like those pasteboard monks which go tumbling one over another, as soon as you tip over the first in the row. Nothing can be drearier than all this prelatical prose, that struts groaning along in its big sleeves, with most elegiac lamentations. Unhappily this melancholy literature generally relieves its insipid commonplaces with now and then a denunciation, and calculates to make the lovers of liberty pay the expense of its tears. It can't afford to cry for nothing.

Very soon the particular question widens out. It is not only the instruction of girls which is on trial, but the whole system of public instruction, both higher and lower. A vast movement for petitioning the government has been organized, all along under the impulse of the Bishop of Orleans, who has touched off the train by his pamphlet on *The Alarms of the Bishops*, in which he passes in review all the symptoms of materialism which alarm him in the instruction of our faculties. Only, by a strange inadvertence, he opens a petition for liberty of instruction, with a demand that the State shall exercise its supervision and repression against such free associations as are guilty of not suiting him. This is the everlasting quibble of the Catholic party. When it talks of liberty, we know that it means nobody's liberty but its own, and that it desires the suppression of other people's liberty. The claw has pricked through the fur quite too often to give us a moment's doubt over its liberal assurances. Have we not seen how it has snatched the first opportunity to secure to its own advantage a monopoly of public education? We should be perfectly agreed with it, if it frankly demanded entire liberty of instruction in all its stages. We are more and more convinced that although the State ought to encourage to the utmost the dissemination of learning, it does not belong to it to do the teaching; for the moment it begins to teach it has to have a doctrine, philosophical, religious, or political, and then we have a State religion, a State philosophy, a State history. We are as much concerned as any one at the encroachments of materialism in education; but it belongs to liberty alone to cure the ills of liberty. Away with all monopolies, and we shall then have no more privileges for any sects. This is all we ask. But the Catholic party wants something very different. It wants to shut the mouths of its opponents, and use the State for a sort of armed servant. Not content with demanding civil repression in the very petition in which it calls for liberty of instruction, it gets up other petitions against popular libraries, which it wants to pick over and expurgate after its own notion; for, according to M. Dupanloup, those are sophists who, like M. Jules Simon, declare that God does not need to be protected by law. Here we see the tip of the ear of this bastard liberalism: and a very dull ear it is; for it has not been able to hear the rules of these libraries, which gave the lie to its accusations in the courts which would fain suspend from their jurisdiction. It reminds us of the ridicule that was heaped, last year, on a certain Dr. Machelard, who made loud and formal complaint to the Senate of some abominable things which he declared that he had heard. The next day it was discovered that this faithful witness was as deaf as a post, and had heard nothing but his own suspicions.

Nothing could have been better contrived for the dishonor of religion than the debate excited in the Senate by the famous petition of the fathers of families. To begin with, the Senate is very conservative toward everything but religion. The bench of cardinals is all very fine to look at, but is a somewhat feebly apostolic body. Doubtless it has had a great deal of experience, such as may be acquired in the service of three or four successive forms of government, but such as does not seem to agree comfortably with a great deal of zeal for the faith. Any religious cause, Protestant or Catholic, carried to the Senate, is sure to cut a sorry figure. The field-marshals who assert the Divinity of Christ while twirling their moustaches or handling their sword-hilts, produce effects rather comic than edifying. As to the cardinals, I appeal to their speeches. Are there many enlightened friends of religion who would not have given something if they never had been delivered? The sole result of these debates in the Senate against materialism and in favor of the true faith, has been to give M. Sainte-Beuve a chance, in his spirited way, to fly out the flag of free philosophy, and to get the laugh on his side—an easy success in the face of such a, blundering enemy. The Minister of Public Instruction confined himself to a timid plea of extenuating circumstances, without one moment rising to the discussion of principles. In fact, he could not do this, for he had no more wish for genuine liberty than his antagonists. He only wanted to get the adoption of a resolution that would not affect the situation.

Nothing remained of all these debates, but irritation and misunderstanding. The anti-religious reaction, alone, found advantage in them. This was the fine conclusion of the grand campaign commenced by my Lord Bishop of Orleans, at a moment when the Encyclical was enough to discredit Catholicism, and therefore Christianity; for in this free-thinking country, Christianity is always confounded with its best known form.

This deplorable campaign of petition to the Senate against public education ought not to shut our eyes to the real state of things, which is, all along, a deep division in the midst of French Catholicism. This division manifests itself especially at Paris. On one side are the religious orders—the Jesuit houses which have been considerably multiplied in the course of these few years, thanks to their unquestionable success in teaching, and especially in fitting students for the great military schools of the government. Around the Church of St. Genevieve there is quite a little world of zealous, facile, religious folk—a sort of Roman colony in the midst of Paris, keeping up here the ultramontane and absolutist traditions. At its head are certain *monsignori* like Mgr. de Ségur, ex-chamberlain to the Pope, who for a long time played the part of a sort of legate, corresponding directly with the Vatican, and giving information as to the doctrine of his ecclesiastical superiors. This disorder has been stopped; the Archbishop of Paris no longer tolerates this inquisition of a subaltern. He has likewise enforced his right to enter the Jesuit institutions, who were disposed to withdraw from his control.

The party of the *zelanti* finds powerful support in the *Faubourg St. Germain*, among the grand families of the legitimist aristocracy. The contrary tendency is very powerful at Paris. The faculty of theology, with its learned dean, Monseigneur Maret, bishop of Sura, belongs to it. We find the same tendency at the archbishop's palace. Monseigneur Darbry is one of the most learned and enlightened of the clergy of the present day. His fine and expressive face bears the seal of distinction and of austerity. He seems consumed by inward fires. His piety is full of impulse, and nothing can be more touching than his allocutions. All ultramontane exaggerations he holds in horror. He has a passionate love for France and her greatness, and groans over the follies which are bringing on a conflict between religion in the future and the spirit of the age. Unfortunately, he is disposed to rely too much on the civil power. He is not satisfied with showing it great deference—he must make it his next friend. His discourse on the occasion of the first communion of the young prince quite exceeded the measure of official respect for the government. This is one side of the old-fashioned Gallicanism which will have to be abandoned at all costs, for religion is more hurt by this attitude of dependence than it is helped by the finest apologetic defences. We express this regret with entire frankness, on the very account of the sympathy we feel for a bishop so well disposed to resist the current of ultramontane follies. He has had much to suffer from the suspicions and the attacks of which he has been the object on the part of the *zelanti*. It is well understood that he is in no good odor at Rome. His personal distinction and eloquence clear up these prejudices, whenever he can plead his own cause before the Pope; but as soon as his back is turned, his detractors get the upper hand again. In reality, there is a fundamental and radical incompatibility between his party and that of his enemies.

The archbishop has brought to Paris, or at least has allowed to grow up about him, a body of young clergy, learned, enlightened, liberal, who would give promise of a noble future yet for the Church of France, if the contrary current were not so strong, and were not favored every day by the highest ecclesiastical authority.

The boldest step of the Archbishop of Paris has been to place in the pulpit of Notre Dame FATHER HYACINTHE, on whom the mantle of Lacordaire has fallen, and who has restored under the vault of the old basilica the grandest days of religious eloquence.

Father Hyacinthe brings to his preaching a generous inspiration, a fiery ardor, which has made him at once a power, and a power of liberty. Born of a literary family, trained in solid classical studies, he entered at an early age into holy orders, and became a Barefooted Carmelite. Men recognized in him, at the outset, the gift of speech in a degree of eminence which placed him in the first rank of orators. His first appearance at Notre Dame was a triumph. The crowds that gather to hear him, stand waiting for two hours before the time. He seems to send over them a breath that lifts them like the waves of the sea. His face is open and intelligent; his voice is sympathetic; he seems ever to be lifted by the movement of his own thought and heart, and at his best moments he has a power of fascination which is absolutely incomparable. The imagination of Father Hyacinthe is beautiful and grand; but it is never more brilliant than when he reproduces the sublime scenes of the scriptural East. Hitherto he has approached only such general subjects as The Personal God, Independent Morality, Civil Society, Religious Society. We are in haste to see him deal with the more direct questions of the religious life which lead directly to the feet of Jesus Christ. The most remarkable thing about his preaching is an admirable liberality with which he recognizes and greets true piety outside of his own Church.

Another trait of his preaching is, that it is as little sacerdotal as possible. He boldly claims the practice of the universal priesthood in the sanctuary of the family. He declares that the father and the mother must exercise the domestic priesthood, and that the great woe of the Church of our day is, that the people of God have abdicated this august charge.

We cite the following fragment from his last winter's conference against Pharisaism.

"Pharisaism, then, in its deepest aspect, is religious blindness:—the blindness of priests who are put in trust with the letter, and who think that the less they explain it, the safer they keep it; a blindness which relates to every point of the sacred deposit; blindness in dogma—the predominance of formula over truth; blindness in morals—the predominance of outward works over inward righteousness; blindness in worship—the predominance of outward rites over religious feeling.

"Blindness in dogma. The Pharisees taught the truth. 'The Scribes and Pharisees sit in Moses' seat,' said Christ; 'believe what they say, but do not what they do.' There is no revealed idea brought to light and quickening the world, but that there is a word to hold it. *Lucerna verbum tuum, Domine.* The Lord's light is in a lamp. But if the word closes itself together, and shuts up the idea as in a narrow and jealous prison,—if it darkens it, stifles it,—that is Pharisaism. This is what the apostle Paul called keeping the truth—but keeping it prisoner in unrighteousness. This is the thing which extorted from the gentle lips of the Saviour Jesus that terrible anathema, *Væ vobis!* 'Ye have taken away the key of knowledge; ye enter not in yourselves, and them that are entering in, ye hinder. Woe unto you!'

"In morals, it is outward works—the multiplicity of human practices, piled up, a miserable and tyrannical burden on the conscience, making it forget, in unwholesome dreams, that it is an honest man's, a Christian's conscience. The Pharisees said to Jesus Christ, 'Why do not thy disciples wash their hands before eating, according to the tradition of the Elders?' And the Saviour answered them, 'Why do ye trample under foot the commandments of God, to keep the commandments of men?'

"But there remains no more religious feeling, when the heart is bending under the weight of outward observances. 'Ah,' said the Lord, 'well did Isaiah prophesy of you, saying: This people honoreth me with lips and hands, but their heart is far from me.'

"Get ye behind me, ye men of the letter! Get ye behind me, ye foes of the human race! *Adversantur omnibus hominibus*, as St. Paul said: 'they are contrary to all men.' And thou, Lord Jesus, arise, my Saviour and my God,—thou who in all thy gentle life wast but twice in anger!—Jesus had no wrath against poor sinners. He sat at their table, and when the adulterous woman fell at his feet, blushing with shame and weeping with remorse, he lifted her, and bade her Go in peace and sin no more. He had no anger against heretics and schismatics; he sat upon Jacob's well, beside the Samaritan woman, and announced to her, with the salvation which is of the Jews, the worship which is in spirit and in truth. But twice was Jesus angry: once, scourge in hand, against those who sold the things of God in the temple; and once, anathema in mouth, against those who perverted the things of God in the law.

"Arise, then, gentle Lamb, in thy pacific wrath, against the enemies of all men, and the real enemies of the kingdom of God—arise, and drive them from the temple!

"Thus it was that the Synagogue perished, and the Christian Church arose.

"We are about to separate, Gentlemen, for one more year. Suffer me, at this moment, to entreat you to unite with me in an act of consecration to this kingdom of God—this Church, whose outer courts we have trodden together. Christianity is not a thing of to-day nor of yesterday. It is not only of the historical epoch of Jesus Christ and the apostles: it is of David, of Moses, of Abraham—it is of Adam, the father, king, pontiff, of us all. In this one religion, then—this Church, whose form may change, but whose foundation abideth unchangeable—ah! Gentlemen, and—suffer me this word, for it is in my heart—friends, brothers, let us consecrate ourselves, as did the prophets, to the love and service of the kingdom of God. The kingdom of God is formally constituted in Christianity, in the Church Catholic, Apostolic, and Roman; but this Church, as I was but just now saying, must ever go on changing from form to form, from glory to glory—*transformamur claritate in claritatem*—until, with all the race of man, it shall have attained the stature of the perfect man in Jesus Christ.

"Yes, Gentlemen, let us love the church in every man, and every man in the church. What matters his condition? Rich or poor, ignorant or learned, *omnibus debitor sum*, I am debtor to every man, says St. Paul. What matters his nationality? Frenchman or foreigner, Greek or barbarian, *omnibus debitor sum*, I answer with Saint Paul,—I am debtor alike to barbarism and to civilization. In one sense, what matters it that we may love the man, what is his religion? If he be not a son of the Catholic church according to the body—the outward unity, perhaps he is —I hope he is—according to the soul—the invisible unity. If he be not a son of the Catholic church according to the soul, nor according to the body—according to the spirit, nor according to the letter—at least he is such in the preparation of God's counsels. If he have not the baptismal water on his brow, I am grieved; but nevertheless I behold there the blood of Jesus Christ; for Christ has died for every man, opening to the whole world his great arms on the cross! The world belongs to Jesus Christ, and therefore the world belongs to the church, if not actually, at least potentially. Let me, then, love every man; and you also, with me, love every man, not only in himself, not only in his narrow and earthly individuality, but in the great Christian community, the great divine community which invites us all."

The soul of a great orator is like an Æolian harp, not inert, but quivering with intelligence and sensitiveness, vibrating with every breeze that blows about it. The conferences of Father Hyacinthe are more than an isolated manifestation; they reveal a condition of the public mind in the midst of which they are uttered. Furthermore, the rage they excite, the vast disdain which the *Univers* affects to cast upon them, add still more to what we may call their *barometrical* value. The Abbé Loyson, brother of the preacher of Notre Dame, brings to the chair of morals in the theological faculty at Paris, a very clear and highly respected liberalism.*

It is true that Father Hyacinthe is succeeded in the pulpit of

---

* This article, although published in October, 1869, was written considerably before the protest of Father Hyacinthe, and the letter of Excommunication of his General.

Notre Dame by Father Felix, who preaches there regularly during Lent. Father Felix is the voice of Jesuitism, a thin, penetrating voice, but not deficient in flexibility. He puts at the service of the Roman doctrine a clear, precise mind, trained to sophistry, capable of taking many an agreeable turn in one direction or another, but always bringing up, at last, with the same genuflexions before the authority of the Pope. Last year he gave two lectures against Protestantism full of gall and injustice, reproducing all the old calumnies. Certainly there is a great contrast between such preaching and the generous accents of Father Hyacinthe; but this contrast is characteristic of the Catholicism of the period.

We should have been glad to open here the chapter of Catholic piety. It would be a very interesting study to trace, in this region of practical life, the two currents which have been conflicting before our eyes in the domain of thought and of the Church. We should have some admirable figures to introduce upon the scene, like some of those, for instance, which are depicted in one of the most affecting books of the day, "A Sister's Story" (*Les Récits d'une Sœur*), by Madame Craven; the beautifully poetic figure of Eugénie de Guérin and that young Catholic theologian the Abbé Péreyve, lately evoked before us by Abbé Gratry, and certainly one of the noblest types of a deep and fervent Christian piety. On the other hand, we should see these waters, so pure at the mountain springs, becoming altered, vitiated, and mingled, in the plain, with the most abject superstitions, such as the pretended miracles of the Virgin of La Sallette and the Virgin of Lourdes—ridiculous but lucrative prodigies, worthy of the charlatan priests of the last days of paganism. We should have to dwell on the development of a new worship, just now in great vogue—the adoration of St. Joseph—which is growing every day, as witness a whole literature of silly devotional writings. Here is something not to be overlooked by those who seek to understand the Catholicism of the present day. In this interesting study, we should have for guide an excellent work, " The Spirit and the Letter of True Piety" (*Sur l'esprit et la lettre de la vraie piété*), by one of the most distinguished young priests of the Paris clergy, Abbé Michaud, who protests energetically against all the abuses of the reviving Pharisaism—against everything which enervates and materializes true religion. But this subject is too important a one to be lightly touched upon. We have only wished to show that the divisions among Catholics are really general and universal, and that they relate to practice as well as to theory.

THE END.

www.ingramcontent.com/pod-product-compliance
Lightning Source LLC
Chambersburg PA
CBHW031745230426
43669CB00007B/494